In Defense of Socialism by Albert Goldman
First Prism Key Press Edition 2012

Prism Key Press
New York, NY 10001
PrismKeyPress.com

ISBN-13: 978-1475029598

In Defense of Socialism

District Court of the United States, District of Minnesota, Fourth Division (27/28 November 1941)

Albert Goldman

CONTENTS

Introduction By Felix Morrow

Albert Goldman's great speech in defense of socialism explains, much better than could an introduction, how we came to be on trial under threat of sixteen-year sentences. A few dates and details, however, are necessary to complete the story.

On June 27, 1941, FBI agents raided the branch offices of the Socialist Workers Party in St. Paul and Minneapolis and carted off large quantities of Marxist literature. On July 15, 1941, an indictment drawn up by the Department of Justice was handed down in St. Paul by a federal grand jury against 29 men and women, including the national leaders of the Socialist Workers Party and sixteen leaders and members of the famous Minneapolis truck drivers union, Local 544.

Why all this in the Twin Cities and not in New York, the national headquarters of the Socialist Workers Party, the Trotskyist movement in the United States? Because on June 9, Local 544, by overwhelming vote of its members, had disaffiliated from Tobin's AFL Teamsters and affiliated to the CIO. On June 13 Tobin had appealed to President Roosevelt for aid, saying

"The officers of the local union were requested to disassociate themselves from the radical Trotsky organization ... these disturbers must be in some way prevented from pursuing this course."

The raids and the indictment followed.

But if the immediate occasion was the inter-union struggle in Minneapolis, the fundamental issue involved was much broader; it was the Socialist Workers Party's revolutionary internationalist attitude toward war and capitalism. As the American Civil Liberties Union concluded,

9

after a careful investigation,

"the Government injected itself into an inter-union controversy in order to promote the interests of the one side which supported the Administration's foreign and domestic policies."

The broader issue dominated the trial which began October 27, 1941. As Albert Goldman's speech demonstrates, the defendants did not merely defend their right to express their anti-war views, took the offensive against the degenerate capitalist system which was prosecuting them. For the first time in this country revolution systematically defended their revolutionary doctrines in a court room, using it as a forum from which to proclaim their ideas.

The false distinction made by the bourgeois liberals – "either persuade the jury or make propaganda for outside" – did not exist for Albert Goldman. He did both together. Naturally, as a revolutionary socialist, his primary concern was with keeping the banner of the revolutionary movement flying and unsullied as an inspiration to the class-conscious workers. But the essential case for socialism is so impregnable, so persuasive, that he could address his revolutionary message also to the jury, as the best possible means winning at least partial concessions from the jury. And that is what happened, as an analysis of the jury's verdict will show.

Of the 28 who went on trial, five were acquitted on both counts by directed verdict of the judge for lack of evidence.

The jury found all 23 defendants not guilty on Count 1, and thus thwarted the government's attempt to use against the labour movement a statute enacted by Congress in 1861 against the southern slaveholders. Count 1 charged violation of the section of this statute which makes it a crime to conspire to overthrow the government by force and violence. Assistant Attorney-General Henry A. Schweinhaut called upon the jury to

10

convict us, because, although the Socialist Workers Party is a small party now, its avowal of the doctrine of the Russian revolution make it possible that, like the Bolshevik Party of Lenin and Trotsky, we could eventually grow to become the leader of a similar revolution here. Thus in acquitting us on Count 1, the jury in effect rejected the government's attempt to transform the 1861 statute into a ban against revolutionary doctrines.

In doing so the jury also in effect characterized the main section of the government's case as a frame-up, for the main purpose of the government's three-week parade of witnesses was to secure a conviction on Count 1 by showing the existence of an immediate conspiracy to forcibly overthrow the government. Under this count the government had pictured the Union Defense Guard of Minneapolis as an army, and had charged that we did "procure certain explosives." This crude police frame-up was rejected by the jury.

On Count 2 the jury found 13 of the 23 defendants guilty but with a recommendation of leniency. That recommendation undermines the moral validity of the guilty verdict. What does leniency imply here? This was no case of crime committed by a youngster under extenuating circumstances. The defendants were obviously in full possession of their faculties, and not a bit remorseful; indignant against their governmental accusers and determined to go on with their revolutionary work. Under these conditions the recommendation of leniency could mean only a formal registration by the jury of its disagreement with the ideas of the defendants rather than a condemnation of the defendants under the criminal law.

The main sections of Count 2 charged that we had conspired to "advise, counsel, urge," and "distribute written and printed matter" to cause insubordination in the armed forces, and "advocate, abet, advise and teach the duty, necessity,

11

desirability and propriety of overthrowing the government by force and violence."

One of these charges – that of insubordination in the armed forces – was so unsubstantiated that it should never have been submitted to the jury at all. The only "evidence" on this point was some oral testimony by two government witnesses to the effect that one or two defendants had told them that soldiers should be induced to "kick" about food and living conditions. Judge Joyce, however, insisted on submitting it to the jury on the ground that "some" evidence had been offered (federal judges may dismiss all or any part of any count in an indictment). The jury, on the other hand, could only vote guilty or not guilty on Count 2 as a whole. Certainly it is hard to believe that the jury recommended leniency if it believed the defendants guilty of causing insubordination in the army.

Even more devastating to the moral validity of the verdict of guilty is the story of what actually happened in the courtroom, which has now been told by certain jurors. There were three jurors who stood ready to vote not guilty on both counts. Had they withstood the pressure, there would have been a hung jury. Instead the jurors, out three days, compromised. Those who believed us not guilty secured acquittal on the first count, acquittal of five on the second count, and a recommendation of leniency, and in return voted guilty on Count 2.

The verdict is a tribute to the persuasive case for socialism made by Albert Goldman. Here were jurors chosen by a hand-picking procedure which made certain that no one known to be sympathetic to labor would be on the venire. They were called upon to pass on a case which, they well understood, had been initiated by the highest circles of the government; an Assistant Attorney-General, sent from Washington, was present to demand of them a guilty verdict. Over the courtroom was the shadow of the impending war – the defendants were sentenced the day Congress declared war, December 8, 1941. Under these conditions it is remarkable that those who believed us innocent were not finally beaten down to submit to a blanket verdict of guilty against all defendants, on both counts, and with no recommendation of leniency.

Judge Joyce sentenced us, some to sixteen months each, the others to twelve months each. We are now out on bail while Albert Goldman and the Civil Rights Defense Committee, with the aid of the American Civil Liberties Union and numerous trade unions, are carrying the appeal to the higher courts.

Meanwhile the case has achieved two triumphs – this great speech and James P. Cannon's testimony, published as **Socialism on Trial**. These inspiring rallying-calls to socialism are worth more than one prison sentence! Read them and get your fellow-workers to do likewise. Albert Goldman will win them not only to our defense but, more important, to the struggle for revolutionary socialism.

I cannot close without a word to the memory of our martyred comrade, Grant Dunne, indicted among the original 29, whom we no longer can save from persecution. He came back from World War I on a stretcher, permanently mangled by wounds and shell-shock. Yet, despite recurrent seizures of this illness, he had a heroic role in leading the hitherto unorganized workers of Minneapolis in great struggles. Shortly before the trial, during such a seizure of illness, worn out by the struggle to defend the workers against the Tobin-Roosevelt onslaught, he committed suicide. Socialism will avenge him, as it will all the innumerable victims of degenerate capitalism.

Thursday, November 27, 1941
Morning Session

The Court: You may proceed, Mr. Goldman.

Mr. Goldman: May it please your Honor, ladies and gentlemen of the jury.

I think that the prediction made in my opening statement, that this would be a case remarkable in many respects, has been confirmed.

In this courtroom there were presented before a jury, ideas, social, political and economic – that have never, to my knowledge, been presented in any Federal Court prior to this case.

Never before, in the history of a Federal Court, has a jury been confronted with the necessity of listening to the social, political and economic ideas and ideals of defendants, formulated in hundreds of articles and pamphlets, for the purpose of determining whether or not the defendants are guilty as charged in an indictment.

A Trial of Heretics

Often, as I sat through this trial, listening to Mr. Anderson reading excerpts, and especially yesterday as I heard Mr. Anderson deliver his argument, my thoughts drifted far afield. What are we in trial for, I asked myself. Certain men wrote books many years go, and we are on trial because these men had ideas and wrote about them. We are on trial because a man by the name of Marx spent most of his lifetime in the library of the British Museum, digging into statistics, statistics concerned with economics and with politics. We are on trial because this man, after reading the mass of statistics, wrote several books in which, taking those statistics as the basis, and analyzing them, he formulated general laws—laws that he thought, and laws that we think, operate in the social system.

We are on trial because a man by the name of Engels and a man by the name of Lenin and a man by the name of Trotsky wrote books, books that have been read by tens of thousands, if not hundreds of thousands of people in this country, and certainly throughout the world.

As I thought about this matter, my mind wandered back into the Middle Ages, and I saw before me inquisitors, prosecutors – their names were not Mr. Anderson, I suppose, but Mr. Anderson could very well have been there – with a heretic standing before them, and these inquisitors were stern and merciless. Lifting up a finger of accusation, the prosecutor said, "He does not believe our doctrine. He does not believe what we have taught for many generations. I accuse him of heresy." And the examination of the heretic began, and perhaps ended by the heretic's recanting, as was the case with the great scientist Galileo, for many feared the punishment of slow torture and painful death.

I do not say, ladies and gentlemen of the jury, that this case is exactly like the cases brought before the inquisition in the Middle Ages. After all, we face only 16 years of imprisonment, while the heretic in the Middle Ages faced torture and death; but essentially the situations are the same. The defendants here are charged with being guilty of heresy. They are guilty because they do not accept the ideas that prevail in society at the present time – Mr. Anderson's ideas. They are guilty because they advocate new ideas which – to use Mr. Anderson's phrase – are capable even of corrupting a saint, should a saint happen to read the literature published by the defendants.

My mind went even further back, into the days of Greece, when an ugly little man, full of wisdom in his head and of gentleness in his heart – Socrates – was accused of corrupting the youth by his ideas and was compelled to take a cup of hemlock.

I think that in essence this trial follows the tradition of the trials of heretics throughout the ages, the trials of people who advocate new ideas, and it is because of this factor, ladies and gentlemen, that I ask you to be doubly and triply careful. When the Court examined you prior to accepting you as jurors, you stated, and I believe with absolute sincerity, that you could and would give us an impartial trial. I have perfect faith that your intentions were and are of the best, ladies and gentlemen. but prejudice is not a garment that can be put on and taken off at will.

Danger of Prejudice

We are here dealing with ideas that are capable of arousing tremendous passion, as you witnessed yesterday when Mr. Anderson spoke; capable also of arousing tremendous zeal in their favor, ideas that actually did arouse millions of men to rise against what they deemed to be injustice; ideas which millions of men thought to be capable of liberating mankind from the ills that confront it. Yes, these ideas can arouse not only zeal and fanaticism, but also tremendous hatred, and they do arouse hatred, because to some people, such as Mr. Anderson, they appear to threaten the very foundations of everything held sacred. I remember that Mr. Anderson, in his opening statement, said that the defendants were conspiring to destroy "organized society." Obviously, what Mr. Anderson designates as organized society, the defendants deem to be completely unorganized, completely chaotic, capable only of destruction and death.

In the indictment the defendants are charged with

conspiring to accumulate and, in fact, the indictment charges that the defendants did accumulate, weapons and explosives. No evidence whatever, of course, was brought to prove that charge in the indictment, unless one considers that the ideas which the defendants have are dynamite. Tyrants of all ages feared the explosive nature of ideas, because ideas are capable of shattering the crust that surrounds the mind of man and of presenting the possibility of a new road, a new life, a new social existence. Ideas, therefore, constitute an explosive far more powerful than TNT, and it is the only explosive that we deal with, the only explosive that the government is capable of proving that we have accumulated.

And I say, ladies and gentlemen, that a human being, no matter how conscientious he may be, no matter how hard he may try to be impartial, must guard himself against prejudices, because prejudices most frequently lie deep in the subconscious mind of a person, and their existence is unknown, even to the person himself.

All of us are obviously born without any prejudices whatever. Have you ever seen a child of one or two or three years of age who knew anything about racial or religious hatreds? I have never seen one, and I know you have never seen one. But as the child becomes an adult, as he absorbs the poisons that exist in modern society, he becomes prejudiced. Every important judgment that a human being makes is determined by the ideas and by the prejudices that he has acquired in his early youth – in school, in church, at home.

The human being cannot get away from his environment. He is chained to it by chains that are not breakable, and most frequently he is chained to the prejudices created by the environment. In a case like this, it is therefore essential to ask yourselves at every step, "Am I permitting my judgment to be colored by my dislike of the ideas of the defendants?" There perhaps is no human being on earth who can get rid of his prejudices completely, but once he is conscious of the fact that he has prejudices, then he can be on guard against them, and being on guard against them, he is more likely, when confronted by new and strange and therefore hateful ideas, to arrive at a fair decision.

It is, of course, impossible for me to give an exhaustive explanation of all the ideas involved in this trial. Thousands of books have been written about them. Perhaps I should have brought some 500 of them into court and asked the judge to permit me to read and discuss all these books; and at the end of a year or two, the jurors could feel themselves more able to pass on the merits of the ideas which we accept.

But I am not here to try to convince you of the justice of our ideas. I am not here to try to show you that those ideas are the only ideas that will solve the problems of mankind. I believe so. My friends, the other defendants, believe so. I am here, however, primarily to explain those ideas sufficiently well so that the issues in this case will become clear to you.

The Indictment

We are charged with conspiracy to overthrow the government by force and violence. We are also charged with conspiracy to advocate the overthrow of the government by force and violence. In order to show you that there is no basis whatever for these two charges, I cannot avoid discussing certain fundamental concepts of ours, concepts brought in by the evidence for the prosecution.

I know that some of you, many of you, have businesses to attend to, and every day is an additional burden. I feel, however, that I have a certain moral right to speak at length because I did not take such a long time to present the case for the defendants; but still I know that it is very difficult for men and women, away from home for four and a half weeks,

19

deprived of their liberty to a certain extent, to sit and listen to an exposition of ideas.

Mind you, there are 23 defendants in this case. In an ordinary criminal case, an hour's final argument for the defendant, threatened with deprivation of his liberty for many years, would certainly not be too much. Don't be scared, ladies and gentlemen, I am not multiplying one hour by 23 defendants. I do not intend to take so much time.

Over 150 exhibits, possibly, have been introduced by the prosecution. I have a right, and perhaps I have the duty, to take every exhibit and comment on it. I shall not do so, not only because it would take too long a time, but because, as I shall explain later, the exhibits will not be of any great aid to the jury in arriving at its verdict.

Above all, it is the importance of the case that justifies lengthy argument. Everyone knows that it is an important case. No matter what your verdict will be, it will go down in history. This will go down in history as one of the greatest trials, not only in the Federal Court of this country, but in the courts of any country.

The Issues in This Case Are Crystal Clear

Permit me first to explain the indictment. In the first count, the charge is that the defendants conspired to overthrow the government by force, and to oppose its authority by force. I do not remember any evidence introduced on that second clause. So that, as to the first count, the jury should concentrate its attention on the question of whether or not we conspired to overthrow the government by force.

The second count has five sections to it. There is a section charging us with conspiring to create insubordination in the armed forces. There is a section charging us with conspiring to distribute written and printed matter that urges insubordination. There is a section charging us with conspiracy to advocate, advise and teach the duty, necessity, desirability and propriety of destroying the government of the United States by force and violence. There is a fourth section charging us with conspiracy to publish and distribute literature advocating the overthrow of the government of the United States by force and violence. And there is a fifth section charging us with conspiracy to organize societies and groups to advocate the overthrow of the government of the United States by force and violence.

But I think all of us will agree, including counsel for the prosecution, that we can confine our attention to three major charges: in the first count, the charge of conspiring to overthrow, and in the second count, the charges of conspiring to advocate the overthrow and to create insubordination in the armed forces.

Immediately upon reading the indictment, the question arises: What is the difference between conspiring to overthrow the government by force and violence and conspiring to advocate the overthrow of the government by force and violence; or what is the difference between those two, and conspiracy to create insubordination?

Let me try, in a few words, to give you my idea of the difference.

It is possible to conspire to advocate to overthrow the government by force and violence without conspiring to overthrow the government by force and violence.

Let me give you an example: One of the persons conspiring to advocate the overthrow of the government may say: "When shall we accomplish our conspiracy?" And someone may answer him, "That is something for the future. In the first place we must advocate, and when we get ready, we'll actually start thinking about overthrowing. That may be in five

21

or ten or fifteen years. For the present we have the task only of advocating." It is, of course, possible to conspire to do both – to advocate and to overthrow – but you can see that it is possible to separate the two.

On the other hand, two or more persons can conspire to overthrow the government without conspiring to advocate the overthrow. That is hardly probable but quite possible.

Conspiring to create insubordination in the armed forces is obviously different from the other two conspiracies. We can assume certain persons disliking the General Staff of the army and wanting to create insubordination in order to get rid of that General Staff. These persons might not at all be interested in overthrowing the government by force and violence.

The difference between the first count and the second count should be kept clearly in mind for it is possible for you to find the defendants guilty of one and not of the other.

Is Our Party a Conspiracy?

At all stages in your deliberations you must ask yourselves the following questions: What charges has the government made against the defendants? What evidence has the government promised in the opening statement of Mr. Anderson to prove those charges? What evidence has it actually produced?

In the first place, it is necessary for you to consider whether or not the defendants are actually guilty of any conspiracy. As Mr. Anderson told you yesterday, if you find that there was no conspiracy, then there is nothing further for you to do. You vote "not guilty," and you are through.

As the prosecution produced its witnesses and introduced its exhibits, two theories appeared to be in the minds of the prosecutors: one, that the Socialist Workers Party is in itself a conspiracy; and two, that the conspiracy was something outside of the party, and the party was only a means for the accomplishment of the conspiracy. According to Mr. Anderson's opening statement, the very purpose of the party, the very plan of the party, the very program of the party and the very activities of the party constitute a violation of the statutes. It would seem, therefore, that the Socialist Workers Party is in itself a conspiracy. That seems to me to be a monstrous proposition. I presume that there are Democrats now in power who think that the Republican party is a conspiracy to take power away from the Democrats. To say that the Socialist Workers Party is in and of itself a conspiracy would mean the beginning of the process of destroying every opposition to those who are in office.

On the other hand, there is the possibility that the government has the theory that the defendants conspired independently of the Socialist Workers Party, that they came to some understanding in some way or other, independently of the party, to create a party for the purpose of advocating to overthrow, or of overthrowing by force and violence, the government of the United States. Is there any credible evidence of such a conspiracy?

It will be necessary for you to choose which theory of the prosecution to proceed on.

Now obviously the term "conspiracy" is altogether inapplicable to this case. I am now thinking of the term, not in the technical, legal sense, but in its generally accepted meaning. A conspiracy is considered to be something secretive, hatched in the darkness of night, with the conspirators fearful lest it should become public. Mr. Anderson tried hard to create that conspiratorial atmosphere in this case. He introduced a floor plan of the party's headquarters. How could it possibly help you to arrive at a conclusion as to whether or not we conspired to overthrow the government by force and violence? But in the

23

mind of Mr. Anderson a conspiracy demands a floor plan, maybe some secret chambers, perhaps some secret buttons. How could it be a conspiracy without a floor plan, without a Sherlock Holmes coming in to study the floor plan?

The prosecution produced evidence that the meetings of the party were held on Thursday nights, and that a membership card was demanded for admission. I presume some of you may belong to organizations that meet on Thursday nights and where only members are allowed to attend. There must be at least 10,000 organizations that permit only members to attend their meetings. Had Mr. Anderson requested it, we would have told him without any hesitation that our membership meetings took place on Thursday nights and that only members were allowed. But had Mr. Anderson done that, it would have destroyed the conspiratorial atmosphere that he has tried to create.

In furtherance of Mr. Anderson's contention that there was a conspiracy, he introduced evidence that our members were known by numbers. It came out during the evidence, however, that the numbers were not given to the members, but were marked on each card. I don't know how many organizations have membership cards with numbers, but there must be plenty of them. But Mr. Anderson wanted to make a conspiracy out of this case, and so he had to transfer the numbers from the cards to the members.

Now then, we come to the final evidence of a real conspiracy! The members were told to destroy the cards. Doesn't that show, asks Mr. Anderson seriously, that these people are conspirators? We admit that the members were told to destroy their cards. This occurred in the Minneapolis branch and did not occur in any other branch throughout the country. The leaders of the Minneapolis branch rightly wanted to protect the rank and file from the kind of persecution that the defendants in this case are subjected to. I admit that Vincent Dunne and Oscar Coover and other leaders of the branch

24

thought seriously of the problem of protecting the rank and file members – not themselves, because they did not conceal their membership. Vincent Dunne testified and told you that he was a member.

There was no attempt by any of the leaders of the party to conceal his membership in the party. Their names were on the editorial staff, or they were openly advertised as speakers for the party. There was, however, a serious attempt to protect the rank and file from being victimized. Does not this case prove that this procedure was correct? We would have been derelict in our duty had we not attempted to prevent victimization of the rank and file members of the party.

The government, by instituting this prosecution, has more than justified this precautionary measure taken by the leaders of the Minneapolis branch. Let the government say that membership in the party is not illegal; let it not indict people who are innocent; and the membership cards will then not be destroyed. But so long as there is the slightest chance that a member of ours will be victimized, so long shall I and other responsible members of the party attempt to protect the rank and file of our party.

Did James P. Cannon or Vincent Dunne or Farrell Dobbs or Grace Carlson deny membership in the party? They want everybody to know that they are members of the party, because they want everybody to accept the principles of the party, but they want also to protect the rank and file members of the party.

In his opening statement, Mr. Anderson claimed that there was no provision in the party's constitution for the withdrawal of a member. My, how terrible this sounds! Once a member, always a member, and one dare not withdraw from membership. But from the testimony of the government's own witnesses you could see that people joined the party and left the party on a purely voluntary basis. Why all this rigmarole about no provision for withdrawal of membership? Because Mr.

25

Anderson wants to create the atmosphere of a conspiracy – a conspiracy that never existed and never will exist.

Every prosecution witness, and Mr. Anderson himself, showed you that instead of being conspirators, we are men and women anxious to proclaim our ideas from the housetops, men and women devoted to our ideas, and extremely interested in getting other people to come to our meetings and to discuss at those meetings. What kind of conspiracy is it when we publish a weekly newspaper and a monthly magazine, when we ask people to come to our meetings, to listen to us and to join our party? Our conspiracy is indeed peculiar; it is a conspiracy that attempts to get the vast majority of the people of the United States to become members of it. We want to convince the majority of the people that they should become as guilty as we are. Open headquarters, open mass meetings, open distribution of literature! Is this characteristic of a conspiracy?

Political propagandists, yes, but don't dare to call us conspirators. Tell the truth. Mr. Anderson, and say that you want us in jail because our ideas are distasteful to you. Tell the truth and say that you want to still our voices, close our headquarters, prevent us from distributing our literature. Don't call us criminal conspirators!

Did we attempt to conceal the organization of the party at the founding conference in December 1937? We would gladly have seen the news of it published in every paper. We published five or ten thousand copies of the party's **Declaration of Principles**. Alas, that we could not publish five million. We got out a weekly paper, a monthly magazine; we issued innumerable pamphlets and participated in political campaigns. You may call it conspiracy in legal phraseology, but please remember that it is a conspiracy only in that sense.

You may, however, be convinced that we are guilty of a conspiracy in a technical, in a legal sense, and it is therefore necessary for me to go on and deal with the object of this alleged conspiracy. You can find that there is a conspiracy, and yet you can easily conclude that we are not guilty if you see that the object of the conspiracy is nothing that is illegal.

Documents Versus Verbal Testimony

Here we must stop a moment to consider the types of evidence introduced by the prosecution. One type is documentary evidence, consisting of articles, excerpts from articles, pamphlets, excerpts from pamphlets, resolutions and excerpts from resolutions; you can read them, study them, analyze them.

Then there is the second type, consisting of statements alleged to have been made by the defendants and testified to by witnesses for the prosecution.

You must keep the distinction between these two types of evidence clearly before you, because it is an exceedingly important distinction, and a great deal depends upon it.

One generalization that almost all people will agree to is that memory is a very treacherous thing. It is the almost universal experience of all lawyers and of all judges that you can hardly ever get ten people who see the same event to testify to exactly the same thing. It is almost a universal rule that, if all ten witnesses tell the same story, they have undoubtedly been coached. If ten witnesses, testifying about a certain speech alleged to have been made a year or two before the testimony, repeat certain statements of the speech in the same way, then it is almost a sure sign that they are falsifying.

It would be horrible to think that a jury would actually find defendants guilty on the basis of evidence of certain statements alleged by witnesses to have been made by the defendants a year or two or three before the trial.

Ladies and gentlemen, do you need any more proof of

that than the fact that the attorneys for the government and the attorneys for the defense disagreed as to what was said an hour after a certain statement was made by a witness? Several times we squabbled about what a witness was supposed to have said the day before. Did I mean to say, when I disagreed with Mr. Anderson, that he was a liar, or did Mr. Anderson mean to say that I was a liar? Not at all. One of us simply did not remember what was said. We always had to go to the record.

But when Mr. Anderson states that he bases his case primarily on the testimony of witnesses who testified to hearing some of the defendants make certain statements a year or two or three years ago, then I am justified in concluding that Mr. Anderson is not dealing fairly with the defendants. Consider the tremendous and terrible possibilities of such a situation. An enemy of yours goes to Mr. Anderson and says: I heard him say he wants to overthrow the government by force and violence. And Mr. Anderson thereupon hauls you before a jury. All that you can say is that you did not make the statement, and the jury may or may not believe you. Can you not see the terrible possibilities in such a case?

I shall show you later that the testimony of the government witnesses is absolutely worthless. It is not only worthless, but most of it consists of downright perjury. But leave that out of consideration. The point that I want to make is that even if you were convinced that the government's witnesses meant to be honest, you should not pay any attention to their testimony of verbal statements alleged to have been made years ago.

The Court: We will have our morning recess at this time.

(Morning Recess)

The Court: You may proceed, Mr. Goldman.

Mr. Goldman: So that, as between documentary evidence and statements alleged to have been made by the defendants and testified to by the government witnesses, it is my opinion that fairness and justice demand that you should exclude the verbal statements.

Which Documents Are Important?

The next question is: Which of the documents that have been introduced should be considered most important?

Counsel for prosecution will undoubtedly say all documents are important and of equal weight but, ladies and gentlemen, here you must take your experiences of life into consideration and base your judgment on those experiences. A mass of about 150 exhibits has been introduced. Articles written by the defendants, pamphlets written by the defendants, articles and pamphlets written by people who are not among the defendants and whom you do not know have been admitted under the rules of evidence as construed by the Court. Then there is the **Declaration of Principles** and there are many official resolutions – all are in evidence.

You have excerpts from pamphlets that were written three or four years ago by persons whom you do not know, have never seen and who are not in the ranks of the defendants. You have articles written in the **Socialist Appeal** and in **The Militant**, in the **New International** and the **Fourth International**, written by people who are not among the defendants.

The question immediately presents itself: Should you

give equal weight to all these documents? Should you, for instance, give as much weight to an official declaration of the party as to an article written by someone who is not among the defendants? It would be absurd not to make a distinction between an official resolution of the party, representing the thought of the most responsible party leaders, and a casual article written by someone whom you do not know and who obviously is not a leader of the party. If he were, he would be here amongst the defendants. Only four of us were brought here from New York to cover up the fact that this case is essentially a prosecution against the leadership of Local 544-CIO, to cover up the real motives of the prosecution.

Then there are other documents in evidence – such as resolutions of the Fourth International. Mr. Cannon testified that we accept them insofar as they are applicable to this country and you should take that testimony into consideration.

It is clear that we didn't keep a staff of lawyers scrutinizing carefully every article that was published in our press with the idea of keeping out anything and everything that might conceivably be used by some federal prosecutor.

Young men, new in the movement, may have formulated certain ideas in a careless manner and not in exact agreement with our **Declaration of Principles** and the prosecution wants to hold the defendants responsible for that, wants to put the defendants in jail because some party members whom you do not know wrote something that might be given a certain interpretation hostile to us. Of course, all these articles are in evidence and from a strictly legal viewpoint you must consider them. But I ask you, ladies and gentlemen, is my request that you should give greater weight to documentary evidence which can be considered as official documents, than to articles written by unknown people, anything but fair and just?

I say therefore that as far as the documents introduced in evidence are concerned, you should give greatest weight of all to the **Declaration of Principles** and the official resolutions of the party. Next in importance come articles written by responsible leaders of the party.

The prosecution has used and will use certain pamphlets for the purpose of trying to get you to bring in a verdict of guilty. Especially is the prosecution interested in having you concentrate your attention on the pamphlet, **Are We for War**, by Draper and the mimeographed pamphlet, **What Is Trotskyism**, by Weber. But I want to point out to you that they were not official declarations of the party. The Draper pamphlet was not even published by the party. The pamphlet, "What Is Trotskyism," was mimeographed – not printed – and it is obvious that this pamphlet was not for popular distribution.

I would be justified in asking you to judge me alone by my own writings and not to condemn the other defendants on the basis of my writings. If there is any rule of law which has been emphasized in Anglo-Saxon tradition, it is that a person must be held responsible for his own acts and not for the acts of others.

It is true that in a conspiracy case the rules of evidence are relaxed and testimony is permitted which is not permitted in other cases but even in a conspiracy case, as fair-minded individuals, you should try to uphold that tradition of Anglo-Saxon law.

I am willing to be judged by my own writings and by the official declarations of the party and by the writings of other responsible leaders, insofar as I agree with them. I do not think that others should be judged by my writings. I am not stating that as a legal proposition applicable in a conspiracy case; I am stating it as a proposition of fairness and justice and not always does the law coincide with fairness and justice. I can see Mr. Anderson trembling at that statement but no one with experience in the law courts can deny that it is the truth.

It would be the greatest travesty of justice if you were to convict people here in Minneapolis on the basis of articles written by persons who are not even defendants and who obviously do not play a leading role in the party.

We didn't sit day in and day out and try to figure out what Mr. Anderson and Mr. Schweinhaut were going to choose from pamphlets, from **The Militant** or the **Fourth International** and present as evidence before the jury. We permitted many people to express their own ideas in their own ways. And everyone who knows anything about editing a paper understands that in the rush of getting copy and sending it to the printer it is impossible to check everything that is written.

Take into consideration all of the documents, but, in all fairness to the defendants, give first place to the official documents – to the Declaration of Principles and official resolutions – and second place to the articles and pamphlets written by the responsible leaders.

The attorneys for the government have read excerpts – an excerpt here and an excerpt there. I could have read excerpts also. How far would it have aided you in coming to your decision? What 1 shall try to give you and in my opinion what you should try to get is as complete a picture as possible of our full program, not an excerpt here or an excerpt there. I shall attempt to give you, by taking the **Declaration of Principles**, Cannon's speeches and my articles and pamphlets and the article of Farrell Dobbs on trade unionism, an analysis of our program. That is all I can do and all I shall try to do. I cannot stop to discuss every excerpt. If an excerpt is read to you by the prosecution, all I can say is: Take it into consideration but remember that it is part of a program. You cannot judge us by an excerpt. You must judge us by the whole program.

I shall skip over lightly and briefly those items in the program which are not very material and immediately proceed to the heart of the questions that have been raised by the prosecution.

The Socialist Society

In the first place it is necessary to get an idea of the fundamental object of the conspiracy charged against the defendants. What is the aim of this great conspiracy? If there is any conspiracy at all, its fundamental object is to get a majority of the people of this country to establish socialism. That is the sum and substance of the conspiracy. If you are interested in finding out the general outlines of what we consider to be a socialist society, you can do so by reading our Declaration of Principles and my pamphlet, "What Is Socialism."

The fundamental feature of a socialist society is that all the means of production – the railroads, the mines, the factories – are owned by the people and the goods that are produced, are produced for use. Under the present system, which we call capitalist, the means of production are owned by private persons or corporations and, although some owners may be very good and charitable gentlemen, they operate their industries not because people need the goods that they produce but because they want to make a profit.

Under socialism the people will decide how many pairs of shoes, how many garments, how many hats, how much coal, how many houses are needed to satisfy the needs of the people and proceed to manufacture them. The productive wealth of society – not goods for consumption such as a coat, or a shirt, or a radio or an automobile – but the productive wealth of society – machinery, factories, mines – will be owned in common by the people, and goods will be produced for the use of the people.

There are no classes under socialism – that is, there is no class that owns the wealth and no class that is exploited. Today a worker has only his labor power and he sells that to someone who owns machinery and he gets a wage in return and the man who owns the machinery makes a profit out of the labor power. That is what socialists term exploitation of labor.

Individuals under socialism will, of course, have different capacities. But no one will be permitted to own any productive wealth and thus exploit labor.

In the final stage of socialism, which some theoreticians designate as communism, the productive forces of society will be so greatly developed and the education of the people will be such as to enable society to follow the principle: From each according to his ability; to each according to his need.

If any one of you raises the objection that human nature makes that impossible, I simply ask you to go to that section of my pamphlet, **What Is Socialism**, which deals with the problem of human nature. Under socialism people will be educated not to think of profit but of service to society. Great scientists even now do not work in their laboratories because they expect to make millions of dollars; they work because they are interested in science.

It will of course be necessary to educate a new generation and it may take time, but given new social conditions it is absolutely certain that it can be done. Given a society that produces enough to satisfy the needs of all human beings, the struggle for the means of life will be abolished. If 12 people have 5,000 apples among them and in addition know that they can get as many more apples as they can possibly eat, there can be no quarrel amongst them for apples. A society that produces enough to satisfy the reasonable needs of people will do away with all the brutal struggles characterizing present-day society.

The Workers' and Farmers' Government

To establish a new social order it will be necessary in the first place to create a new government which we call by the name of workers' and farmers' government. You can see that I am only touching on essentials. I haven't the time to do any more. What will be the duty of that government? To take over the means of production now owned by capitalists and begin operating them for the benefit of the people; and also to begin the education of a new generation to transform the human being from what he is under capitalism into what he will be under socialism.

The workers' and farmers' government is technically called a dictatorship of the proletariat. When that phrase is uttered by Mr. Anderson or Mr. Schweinhaut it sounds terrible. The defendants are in favor of dictatorship! Of course it is nothing but a technical term indicating simply that the government representing the workers and farmers will take the productive wealth away from those who own it today, from the Sixty Families and their satellites. To that extent it will be a dictatorship. A dictatorship of the vast majority over the very small minority.

Will this "dictatorship of the proletariat" be a democracy or a dictatorship in the usually accepted term? Read page 8 of exhibit 1 – our **Declaration of Principles** – and you can see that the term "dictatorship" as commonly used is not applicable to the dictatorship of the proletariat. That section reads as follows:

"While the workers' state will necessarily reserve to itself the indispensable right to take all requisite measures to deal with violence and armed attacks against the revolutionary regime, it will at the same time assure adequate civil rights to opposition individuals, groups, and political parties and will guarantee the opportunity for the expression of opposition through the allotment of press, radio and assembly facilities in accordance with the real strength among the people of the opposition groups or parties."

That goes far beyond the democracy that exists at

35

present. A workers' and farmers' government will not only permit free speech and free press and free assembly in the abstract but will see to it that a minority will have the means to exercise that free Democracy to a certain extent exists under the present regime. consider the essence of the question: If workers have the constitutional right to publish a paper but lack the funds with which to do so, then their right is an abstract one. On the other hand, the right of an individual who has sufficient money to publish a chain of papers is a real one.

The rights under capitalist society granted by the government representing capitalist interests are, by and large, abstract rights. A famous French writer, Anatole France, expressed this idea as follows: "Under capitalism rich and poor are equal. They both have the right to starve in the streets." The difference is that only the poor man exercises that right to starve.

When the term dictatorship of the proletariat is mentioned, you must not think of it as a dictatorship of Hitler or Stalin. Trotsky began a struggle against Stalin because of the very fact that Stalin transformed the dictatorship of the proletariat into a personal or a clique dictatorship. Under the dictatorship of the proletariat there will be far, far greater democracy than has ever existed on the face of the earth.

Our Attitude Toward Governments

We come now to the heart of the question, the question of whether or not we are guilty of conspiring to overthrow the government by force and violence. As the evidence shows, the main object of our so-called conspiracy is to establish a socialist society. How do we intend to do that? That is the main question at issue.

As I shall attempt to show you, all other questions— such as our attitude on war, on trade unionism, our military policy – are subsidiary. The question of guilt or innocence must be determined on the main issue and not on the subsidiary issues. But it is impossible to decide the main issue without considering certain fundamental concepts of socialism.

In the first place, let us get clear what is meant by the term government. Let us not be awed by an abstraction. Men and women elected or appointed to office and having prerogatives constitute this thing we call government. These men and women are not any more gifted than you or I. They have certain authority. Sometimes they abuse that authority – very frequently they do so. Place a man in a position of power and the chances are that he will take advantage of his position and exercise his authority at any and all opportunities. Some people in authority remain courteous; others are corrupted by it.

The phrase, destruction or overthrow of the government, raises in most minds a terrible picture of the use of weapons and violence. But you can see that to abolish or destroy or overthrow a government can mean and usually does mean, replacing certain individuals, organized in a certain way, basing themselves on certain concepts, replacing them with other individuals, organized in a different way and basing themselves on different concepts.

"Whenever any form of government becomes destructive to these ends the people have a right to alter or abolish it and institute a new government in a form most likely to effect their safety and happiness." The writers of the Declaration of Independence who formulated the horrible idea that the people have a right to abolish a form of government are not amongst the defendants. The words "overthrow, abolish, destroy" do not necessarily connote violence. They simply mean that the people using those words want to change the government so that it will be based on entirely new principles.

We use the term "capitalist government" – a terrible phrase to some people. Does it mean that all those who are

37

elected to Congress or to any executive or judicial office are themselves financiers and capitalists? No, it simply means that the government which we call capitalist bases itself upon the rights of private property in the means of production and does everything in its power to protect those rights. Essentially, a capitalist government is a government which has as its main function the protection of the existing property relationships.

There are different types of capitalist government – some conservative, some liberal. As you know, Roosevelt and some people in his government have been called communists. That, of course, is absurd but it proves that if one does not like a person or does not agree with his policies, it is a good idea to call him a communist. Though some people call the Roosevelt administration communist, we designate it by the term capitalist. It is a capitalist government by virtue of the fact that private property in the means of production exists and the government protects the rights of private property in the means of production.

You must remember that what we are interested in primarily, as is shown by the evidence, is not to change the government, but the social system upon which the government is based. We call the present social system capitalist because men are permitted to own productive wealth and to hire and exploit wage labor.

We want a socialist society where all the productive wealth is owned in common and there is no exploitation. What type of government do we want? That is a question of secondary importance. If, for instance, socialism could be introduced under the present form of government – with the two Houses of Congress, the Executive, the Judiciary – we would have no objection.

In our **Declaration of Principles** you will find proposals for occupational representation. Instead of having representatives from certain territories, we think it is best for the workers and farmers to elect their representatives directly from factories and from the farms. We believe in the principle of occupational representation because we think that anyone elected by his fellow-workers or fellow-physicians or fellow-scientists, is far more likely to represent the real interests of his group. There will be no representation of lawyers under socialism because lawyers are a plague that will no longer exist in a socialist society.

Under a workers' and farmers' government there will be one house of congress instead of two. Our present form of government operates on the principle of checks and balances. The Senate checks the House of Representatives, the President checks both Houses of Congress and then the Judiciary has a check on both the Executive and the Legislative branches. This, in our opinion, is far from democratic and was instituted primarily to prevent the masses of people from exercising their will in the matter of legislation.

Originally the senators were elected, not by a direct vote of the people but by the legislators of the different states, thus enabling the wealthier citizens to get into the Senate of the United States. Later on, by an amendment to the Constitution, the senators had to be elected by the people. We, on the other hand, want a complete revolution in the form of government. We want a government organized in such a way that it can best serve the interests of the producers. I know that the term "revolution" sends shivers down the back of Mr. Anderson and he hopes that the same shivers will run down the backs of the jurors. But remember that the term "revolution" does not necessarily imply violence.

I think the Court will define that term for you – a definition as is found in Webster's dictionary. It simply means a radical change and social revolution means a radical change in society. Do we not speak of a revolution in science, a revolution in transportation? We even speak of a revolution in women's dresses.

Marxist Conception of Society

We want a social revolution; that is undeniable. By that we mean that our aim is to transfer the economic and political power from the class we call capitalists to the workers and farmers. When that happens, a social revolution will have occurred.

The French revolution, as Mr. Cannon correctly testified, was a social revolution because the merchant and capitalist class displaced the feudal class. The power to rule society was transferred from the landowning feudal nobility to the merchants and industrialists.

There may be political revolutions that are not social revolutions. The revolutions that occur frequently in Latin America are political revolutions because they do not change the social system.

A social revolution may or may not be accompanied by violence and no one knows exactly how it will occur in the future.

Marxists are of the opinion that society operates on the basis of certain laws. It is important for you to understand that basic idea. I do not ask you to agree with our concept of society, but I do ask you to understand what our concept is. For if you realize that we believe that certain laws operate in society, independent of our will and of your will and of Mr. Anderson's will, you will see that it would be impossible for us to conspire to overthrow the government by force and violence. The responsibility for a revolution lies not upon us but upon the very nature of the social system in which we live.

Some of you might have heard or seen in print the phrase, "economic determinism." It is not the theory of socialism, but it does give you an idea that socialists consider the economic factor the determining factor in the development of society.

The primary concern of human beings has always been to feed, clothe and shelter themselves. As human beings lived together, certain necessities drove them to invent certain machines and with the invention of these machines production increased and with the increase in production changes occurred in the economic and social system.

Struggles arose between groups and the victors made slaves out of the vanquished. A system of slavery arose and the forces of production continued to develop.

More machines were invented; the forces of production increased; society developed further and ever further and class struggles arose; slaves revolted against masters; the social system based on slavery could no longer function effectively and that social system was displaced by a new system.

What is known as feudalism came into existence. He who owned land had the right to exploit the man who worked on the land and this man who worked on the land was called a serf. In comparison with the chattel slave, he was a free man but nevertheless he could not leave the land.

The discovery of America gave a tremendous impetus to the development of industry; new markets came into being; new machinery was invented; the forces of production grew and with it a new and powerful class arose – the merchant class of the Middle Ages – and it is this merchant class that constituted the beginning of modern capitalist class. We call that class the "bourgeoisie" and this class began a struggle against the feudal nobility and finally conquered and became the dominant class in society.

Thus you see that, in our opinion, a class struggle has existed since time immemorial. The chattel slaves struggled

41

against the masters, the plebeians struggled against the patricians, the serf against the feudal nobility; and today we have the fundamental struggle between the capitalists who own the wealth and the wage workers who create the wealth. And is this struggle a result of man's will or desire? No, it is a struggle that is due fundamentally to the development of economic forces. A social system is born, develops, decays and is displaced by a new social system – all this by virtue of laws at operate independently of the will of human beings.

A new social system gives birth to new ideas, to new moral concepts. Under the feudal system in the Middle Ages, for instance, the church prohibited the lending of money on interest. To lend money on interest was considered usury. But with the development of the merchant class and the capitalist system, the lending of money became an absolute necessity and obviously people would not lend money unless they could make a profit out of it. The rule of the church against usury was abolished and interest up to a certain point was permitted.

Man's ideas, man's morals, man's philosophies are determined fundamentally by the economic structure of society and not vice versa. The history of man is determined not by his will nor by his consciousness nor by what he thinks is right or wrong but by inexorable economic forces operating on the basis of certain laws.

This idea was first introduced by Karl Marx, and the defendants, considering themselves Marxists, accept that idea, and accepting that idea you can see that the factors which they consider primary in the creating of a social revolution are economic factors. All that we can possibly do is to indicate that the economic forces of society are moving in a certain direction and that the masses of the people must also move in that direction.

Society cannot be changed by the mere desire of a small group to change it. It must, in the first instance, be ripe for a

42

change and in the second instance the masses of men must understand the necessity for a change.

We have now reached a point in the development of society where mankind must take control of social forces and determine the operation of those social forces. Up to now, man has been subjected to social forces that he did not understand and could not cope with. What man must do now is to become master of his own destiny. If man does not do so, then fascism, barbarism, the destruction of all liberties and of all culture will inevitably follow.

Look at our social system and you can see for yourselves how the class struggle operates. The tenant farmer struggles against the landlord, the sharecropper against the southern plantation owner, the worker against the employer, farmers and workers together against Wall Street. Why is our society subjected to these struggles? Because each social group wants a larger share of the income that society produces.

Of all the struggles existing in modern society, the one between the industrial wage worker and those who own the industries is the bitterest and most virulent. It is the fundamental struggle of our epoch.

That is not our responsibility, ladies and gentlemen. In comparison to the number of wage workers, our party constitutes a small group; the class struggle goes on without us.

Unfortunately we have not as yet achieved an influence which can permit us to play a decisive role in that struggle. Mr. Anderson is anxious to prevent us from achieving that influence and that is why he asks you for a verdict of guilty. But I can assure Mr. Anderson that the class struggle will go on even if we should be in jail. The coal miners are on strike now. We have nothing to do with it. We had something to do with Local 544 in Minneapolis and that is why we are defendants in this courtroom. But the struggle between the teamsters and the

43

Minneapolis employers is only a tiny section of the class struggle that goes on constantly throughout the United States. That struggle goes on whether Mr. Anderson and Mr. Schweinhaut like it or don't like it.

The struggle between the worker on the one hand, anxious to get a higher wage, and the employer on the other hand, anxious to make more profit, is a struggle that will go on regardless of the desire or the intention of any man. There are some employers who are willing to give higher wages but they are prevented by the law of competition under capitalism. By and large the employers are anxious to make more and more profits and, because of that, the class struggle must necessarily continue.

The Court: We will have our noon recess at this time.

Thursday, November 27, 1941
Afternoon Session

When Men Can Be Good

The Court: You may proceed, Mr. Goldman.

Mr. Goldman: Throughout history there have been men who dreamed of changing society. They saw the poverty, the oppression, the persecution and hatred that prevailed in the world and concluded that the only way by which these evils could be abolished was to have men accept the right kind of beliefs. The prophets of old, Christ, the philosophers of the Middle Ages thought they could change society by teaching men to be good. If only people actually practiced the Commandments!

Then came Karl Marx who presented the startling proposition that to change man, you must change the social system. It is impossible to have a society where love between human beings prevails, unless you have a society where the struggle for economic existence is done away with. Under the present social system, mean, petty and violent struggles prevail in all classes. Way up on top there are struggles for colonies and spheres of influence; then there are struggles in the form of bitter competition between business men; there are struggles between the small business men and the chain stores; there are struggles between workers. Everywhere in society struggle prevails.

There are some people who claim that the human being is essentially bad and no attempt to change his nature can succeed. But when one considers that in spite of the meanness and violence that prevail in society, there are millions of decent human beings, one must come to the conclusion that the human being is essentially good.

Marx concluded that before man can develop to a point where the relationship between one human being and another will be on a decent basis, society will have to be altered. Under the present social system all moral codes and all ethical concepts are accepted, by and large, only in words. People believe in religion, believe in the Fatherhood of God and the Brotherhood of Man and yet they kill one another by the millions.

Marx formulated the following proposition: that the ideas, the philosophies, the religions and the morals of a certain epoch are determined fundamentally by the prevailing social system; change the social system and the ethical codes and philosophies will also change.

Decline of Capitalist System

There are certain diseases in youth which are latent and not until old age sets in does the individual become aware of their existence. The human body has powers of resistance which decrease with old age. Germs which have no ill effect in early age become very dangerous in later stages in life.

Thus it is with the capitalist system. During its youth the contradictions existing within it were easily overcome. In this country, or instance, there were vast stretches of land available for agriculture and settlement; factories could be and were built; railroads were developed. But as the land was occupied and more and more factories were built, it became more difficult for the capitalist system to function. The economic crises which were easily overcome in the early stages of the capitalist system of this country became more serious until in 1929 a crisis came that shook the very foundations of the country.

Throughout the world the capitalist system is in a stage

of decline. Old age has set in and the contradictions inherent in the capitalist system have become acute. Unemployment, fascism, catastrophic wars – these are the diseases that afflict capitalist society in its days of decline. Are the defendants responsible for that? Not in the least!

This country is capable of producing tremendous quantities of goods to satisfy, beyond all imagination, the needs of the people. But the industries, under the present economic system, cannot function for peace, for life – they function only for death. The industries that were more than 50 per cent idle in peacetime, when men needed food, clothing and shelter, are now running full blast, producing planes, bombs and dreadnoughts.

And in this period of capitalist decline people are dissatisfied and fascism appears on the scene and takes advantage of their dissatisfaction. The fascists, claiming to create a new order, are actually throwing the world back toward barbarism. Everything that man has produced that is worthwhile is destroyed by this monster of fascism. The existence of this monster, however, is not to be attributed to Hitler or Mussolini – to ill-will the of one or two or a dozen men – it is to be attributed to the decline of the capitalist system. Capitalism has reached a point where mankind must take control of the productive forces and begin producing goods for the use of the people – and this means socialism – or else it will be hurled into the abyss of fascism and destruction. This is our belief and this is what we teach.

But how will this change from capitalism to socialism come about? Here we come to the heart of the case.

Do we advocate the idea that people should take up arms and destroy the government and thereby bring a change in the social system? By the destruction of the government is necessarily meant, according to Mr. Anderson, the destruction of the people who represent the government and the army and navy.

From the very beginning of the socialist movement there have been struggles around the question as to the best method of changing the social order. Marx fought vehemently against the anarchists, who declared that no government at all is necessary and that every form of government is hostile to the masses.

Then there was a controversy between Marx and a Frenchman by the name of Blanqui, who insisted that a social revolution required only a courageous, armed small group. Marx declared that the liberation of the people is the task of the people themselves and not the task of a few agitators, no matter how determined and courageous. The majority of the people must understand what is necessary and must be willing to struggle to achieve their liberation.

In the **Communist Manifesto**, written by Marx and his collaborator Engels, the fundamental ideas of socialism were first formulated. That book was introduced into evidence by the government against the defendants. In that book there is found the following statement:

"All previous historical movements were movements of minorities or in the interest of minorities. The proletarian movement is the self-conscious, independent movement of the immense majority in the interest of the immense majority."

Marx therefore accepted two fundamental principles: one, the necessity of convincing the majority of the people to accept the ideas of socialism, and two, the necessity of establishing a government that will begin building the socialist society.

We Aim to Get a Majority

Mr. Anderson read an article of mine which I introduced into evidence just before closing the case for the defense. It was published in **The Militant** of March 29, 1941.

In order to prove that we did not believe in convincing a majority of the people, Mr. Anderson showed that sometimes I used the term "majority" without mentioning the people and at other times I used the term "majority of the working class."

What do I mean when I use the phrase "the majority of the working class"? Read the section that I have already cited from the **Communist Manifesto**. Read in my pamphlet, **What Is Socialism**, that section where I state specifically that there are probably no more than three million people who can be considered capitalists in the United States. Read that section in my pamphlet which says that the working class in an industrially developed country like the United States constitutes a majority of the people. And then read that section where I say that the workers, even though they are in a majority, must have the help of the middle classes, especially of the farmers, in order to achieve victory, and you will see that I cannot mean what Mr. Anderson says I mean, that is, a majority of only one class, a minority of the people.

The industrial wage workers are the ones to take the lead in the struggle against the capitalist system. In the first place, they come more directly in conflict with the owners of industry – in the big steel mills, auto plants, mines, etc. In the second place, the industrial wage workers are used to working together – cooperation is the key word under socialism and the industrial wage workers in their factories learn to work cooperatively. They understand that it is necessary under conditions of modern industry to work cooperatively in order to build an automobile or a complicated machine.

The farmer, on the other hand, working on his own land, tends to be individualistic. It is necessary for the workers to get the support of the farmers. In my pamphlet I state that in a socialist society the farmers will finally come to realize the advisability of cooperative farming. The point that I want to

49

emphasize is that whenever we use the expression "the majority" or "the majority of the people" or "the majority of the working class" we mean one and the same thing – the same thing that I read to you from the **Communist Manifesto**:

"All previous historical movements were movements of minorities or in the interest of minorities. The proletarian movement is the self-conscious, independent movement of the immense majority in the interest of the immense majority."

I am certain that, if the government in this case were simply interested in bringing into court possible violators of a law, it would have moved for a dismissal of the case immediately upon learning that the Socialist Workers Party aims to get a majority of the people to accept its ideas. If counsel for the government did not know our position before, they should by now have wired Washington for permission to dismiss the case because the phrase *majority of people* settles all questions as far as our guilt of advocating the violent overthrow of the government is concerned.

I presume, ladies and gentlemen, that you do not think the defendants are insane. You may not agree with us; you may think that we are utopians, but I believe you consider us sane people. Only insane people, however, would be capable of actually preferring and desiring violence. If there is an individual who says that he wants a violent overthrow of the government, a violent transformation from the capitalist system to the socialist system, he belongs in the insane asylum.

And if, as is shown by our writings, we want a majority of the people to accept our ideas, why should we advocate a violent change from capitalism to socialism? What does advocate mean? To incite, to urge. We would then be convicted of saying: Even though we get a majority of the people behind us, we still want to overthrow the government by violence. The fact that we want a majority of the people to accept our ideas proves beyond all doubt that we want a peaceful transformation.

50

I want to repeat this fundamental proposition because it is all-important. If we want a majority of the people, as we do, to accept our ideas, then we must be in favor of a peaceful "destruction" of the government. Does peaceful destruction sound paradoxical? Not if you understand it correctly in the sense that it means the removal of certain persons ruling on the basis of certain principles, and replacing them by other persons obligating themselves to rule upon different principles. When government counsel failed to stress the fact that the Socialist Workers Party desires to have a majority of the people on its side, it could only he explained on the hypothesis that Washington in this case was out for a conviction regardless of the evidence.

The only interpretation that honest people can accept of the idea of violence as contained in our program is the following: We predict that even after a majority of the people is won over to the ideas of socialism and tries to establish socialism peacefully, the minority, organized by the capitalists, will resist with violence. Especially is that true now, because of the rise of fascism.

The Prosecution Distorts Our Ideas

One factor that you must take into consideration and always be on your guard against, is the possibility of distortion by excerpts. A person writes an article, ,a party formulates a program based on fundamental theories. Along comes a prosecutor and snatches an excerpt here and a sentence there. The possibility of distortion is very great.

"Think not that I am come to bring peace on earth. I come not to bring peace, but the sword. And the son shall be set against the father, and the daughter against the mother, and the daughter-in-law against the mother-in-law."

Is not the one who wrote these two verses an advocate of

51

violence and hatred? If Mr. Anderson did not know that the Prince of Peace uttered these words, he probably would seek to indict the author.

Every piece of great literature can be distorted. The Bible can be made into an obscene book simply by taking out certain excerpts. This is the method which the jury must guard against. Excerpts can be found from the writings of Karl Marx, from our program, from Trotsky, from Lenin, which would indicate that we want and we advocate a violent revolution, but that would be false, that would be a distortion, because taking the program as a whole, it is clear that we want to gain a majority of the people to our ideas, and from that it follows that we want to gain power peacefully.

Will there be struggle at the time the majority decides to establish socialism? I told you before that in this society struggle is an unalterable law. At times the struggle is on a political plane, at times it is on an economic plane. Workers join together, create a union, try to get a raise in wages or an improvement in conditions, and struggle follows.

And sometimes that struggle is accompanied by violence. That is true not only of a strike of truck drivers in Minneapolis. Read the history of the labor struggles in the United States, of great strikes in Colorado, in southern Illinois, in Ohio and elsewhere, and you will convince yourselves that violence is not something that occurs in strikes led by Trotskyists. In 1877, at a time when socialists were never heard of outside, perhaps, of New York City, there were great railroad strikes, and violence resulted. What caused the violence? The agitation of some people? No. The bitter struggle between exploited workers and greedy employers.

Unfortunately, we are compelled to say that in all probability the social revolution will be accompanied by violence. Do we therefore advocate violence? No. We want a peaceful transformation.

There have been civil wars in history. History does not know of a single case where a ruling group, controlling economic and political power, has peacefully surrendered that power to a majority. Perhaps we have entered a period when the ruling class will realize that it is useless to struggle and will surrender its power without violence. We hope so; we hope that the ruling class in this country, when confronted by a majority determined to establish a new social order, will see the advisability of giving in peacefully. But we do not want to create that illusion; and that is what we mean in our Declaration of Principles when we say it is an illusion that socialism can be introduced through parliamentary means. It simply means we believe that after we gain a majority of the people to our ideas, the ruling group will not surrender peacefully.

Our Rights Were Won by Struggle

Theoretically, the existence of political democracy offers a chance to achieve socialism in a peaceful manner. But even the democratic rights that we have now have not been gained without struggle.

Do you think that everyone had a right to vote in the early stages of the republic? No, there were property qualifications attached to the right to vote. A struggle began to abolish these qualifications. Mass agitations, mass demonstrations were utilized in that struggle. People were jailed in that struggle, but finally they won the passage of laws granting the right of suffrage to every person without any property qualifications. But go down into the South and you will find that the Negroes still do not have the right to vote.

Take the principle of compulsory free education. Do you think that was gained without tremendous agitation that lasted for years and decades? Read the history of our country and you will see differently. Nothing, nothing of value that mankind possesses has been achieved without sacrifice, without struggle.

53

The prosecutors point to our literature which speaks about mass demonstrations and mass agitation. We do not deny that we believe in the effectiveness of mass demonstrations. The prosecutors must have forgotten that in the history of this country many things have been won by mass demonstrations.

We are now in a period when the people should have real democracy, economic and political, and a struggle will be necessary in order to achieve that. It will be waged on the political field; it will be waged in strikes against employers; it will be waged in debates, mass demonstrations, in the courtrooms, and people will be jailed.

We Shall Try to Avoid Violence

On the basis of their analysis of history and social conditions, Marxists predict the future. Will we be right? No one knows. I hope, and I am certain that every one of my co-defendants does, that our prediction with reference to violence accompanying the social revolution will not be fulfilled.

We want to take over the means of production peacefully, but we predict that the minority will use violence to prevent the majority from achieving a peaceful transformation, and it is necessary to be ready for the violence of that minority.

We are not able to predict with great exactness. A social scientist cannot predict with the exactitude of a physical scientist. What we can say now, however, is that as the ideas of socialism gain ground, as more and more people become convinced that socialism is the only possible solution, the fascists will also gain strength. In Germany the fascists were financed by the big industrialists. The capitalists in this country will do the same. They will finance the fascists to destroy the labor movement. The only real possibility of avoiding violence is for the working masses and the farmers to organize so strongly that the minority of capitalists will not attempt the use of violence.

The fact that we support the formation of a labor party is an indication that we shall try our best to exhaust all possibilities for peaceful change. To Mr. Anderson our support of a labor party evidence of a plot. To him it means that we would like to see a labor party so that the dupes in that party will participate in elections while we, behind the scenes, plot to overthrow the government by violence. What utter nonsense!

Mr. Cannon said on the witness stand that, as serious political people, expecting the masses to accept our ideas, we cannot conceal those ideas. We cannot say or do one thing and expect that the masses will be able to read our minds and follow us in doing something else. According to Mr. Anderson, we organized a union defense guard in order to overthrow the government by force and violence. But he never proved, because he never could prove, that we ever told that to the members of the union defense guard. Presumably, then, we would call together the union defense guard one fine morning and reveal the startling secret to them that they are expected to overthrow the government by force and violence. Is it not absurd to think that we expect people to follow us in an attempt to overthrow the government when we have never told them that such was their duty?

Our task is to inform the masses of our ideas. We cannot possibly be conspirators, because we want to educate the majority of the people to accept our ideas. There is a section in our **Declaration of Principles** which says specifically that our task is to convince the masses that our ideas and our solution to the problems of mankind are correct and that it is impossible to use force against the masses. We can use only the power of persuasion and no other power.

Through a labor party we attempt to educate the masses to act independently on the political field and also to exhaust all possibilities of a peaceful change. We do not claim that the creation of a labor party will assure a peaceful change. We are against creating illusions because even if a labor party is created, the probability of the capitalists' organizing a minority to prevent a peaceful change remains the same. And we are not afraid to tell the masses exactly that, and it is not against the law to say so. It is against the law to incite and urge people to overthrow the government by force and violence, but it is not against the law to predict that violence will be used by the minority to thwart the will of the majority. And this is the crux of the question, ladies and gentlemen.

On the basis of the evidence you can find only that, basing ourselves on an analysis of history, on an analysis of the social forces operating in present society, we declare that the probability is overwhelming that the social revolution will be accompanied by violence – the violence of the minority determined to guard its rights, its powers, its privileges.

I think – I am certain – the Court will instruct you that if, in considering all of the evidence in the case, you conclude the evidence may just as well be consistent with the innocence of the defendants as with the guilt of the defendants, you are under an obligation to accept the hypothesis of innocence. That is the law.

Let us assume that after listening to all of the evidence and all he arguments in this case, and after reading all of the exhibits, you say to yourselves that the evidence can be interpreted in two ways: one, that the defendants advocated the violent overthrow of the government, and the other that the defendants predict there will be violence. Then you must accept the latter hypothesis and find us not guilty.

Minority Responsible for Violence

Mr. Cannon pointed out under cross-examination by Mr. Schweinhaut some historical examples where the majority won the power peacefully, but where the ruling minority initiated violence and began a counter-revolution. One example is our own Civil War where, after Lincoln was elected by the people, the southern slaveholders began the revolt. The slaveholders refused to give up their privilege of owning chattel slaves and fought to extend slavery. Violence began, but it came from the South, from the minority, and it was not until the majority of the people residing in the North assembled all their forces that they were able to put down the slaveholders' revolt.

Who was responsible for the violence? A minority of slaveholders determined to hold on to their property rights against the majority of the people.

I presume there were many people who, prior to the Civil War, predicted that violence would accompany the abolition of slavery. Were they responsible, then, for the Civil War? Is the Civil War of a clear example of a peaceful accession to power and the use of violence by a minority to overthrow the majority?

In Spain we have another example. The Loyalist government had the support of the vast majority of the people and came to power because of the support of the people. The fascists thereupon organized their minority, and with the aid of Germany and Italy, began a violent counter-revolution and succeeded in defeating the majority.

On the basis of these historic examples and many others, on the basis of the present-day struggles in industry, where the employers do not hesitate to use violence to prevent workers from organizing unions to improve their working conditions, we predict that the social revolution, which will have as its aim to take away the wealth and the power and the privileges of a small minority, will be resisted by that minority to the death.

The more we emphasize that possibility, the more the people understand that possibility and prepare for it, the less will be the violence. But if violence does come, will we be responsible? Is the weather-man responsible for predicting a hurricane? Is the physician responsible when he predicts death for the patient? Is the astronomer responsible when he predicts the coming of an eclipse? Are we, predicting a great social storm at the time of the social revolution, responsible for the violence that may ensue?

A great deal has been made by the prosecution of the fact that in our writings appears the statement that we intend to take advantage of a revolutionary situation. What is that revolutionary situation? The only government witness who attempted to explain it, Bartlett, went way beyond his depth. He may be a shrewd union business agent, but he is hardly capable of explaining the theoretical problems connected with socialism.

The prerequisites for a revolutionary situation have been summed up by Marxists to be the following: First and foremost is the decline of the social system when the forces of production can no longer function effectively; second, the inability of the ruling class to solve the problems it is confronted with; third, great suffering of the masses; fourth, the desire and determination of the masses to change the social system; fifth and final, existence of a party trained to understand the operation of social forces, able to predict the direction in which society moves, and determined not to permit a minority to thwart the will of the majority.

Mr. Cannon correctly explained to you that these conditions do not as yet exist in the United States. Much has been said here by the prosecution to the effect that the defendants believe that the war will create a revolutionary situation. Perhaps it will, ladies and gentlemen, but are we responsible for the war? And if the war does create a revolutionary situation, can we be held responsible for the revolutionary situation? Perhaps the prosecution – and by the prosecution I do not mean Mr. Schweinhaut or Mr. Anderson, but Washington – should busy itself with passing a law preventing the war from creating a revolutionary situation. Or might I suggest that in order to prevent the possibility of a revolutionary situation, the present administration refrain from going to war.

The Court: We will take our afternoon recess now.

(Afternoon Recess)

Advocacy of Violence – Or Prediction

The Court: You may proceed.

Mr. Goldman: The distinction between prediction and advocacy should by this time be perfectly clear. But that does not seem to be the case as far as government counsel are concerned. They introduced into evidence my pamphlet **What Is Socialism** and read an excerpt from it beginning with page 33. This is the pamphlet that I handed out to you at the beginning of the trial and if you have read it, you probably saw that it was written in very simple language because it consists of a series of lectures delivered to workers. It is under such conditions that the clearest exposition of our thought is necessary because when one speaks to workers he is compelled to reduce his ideas into the simplest terms. On page 33 I asked the following question: "What methods will the workers be compelled to use in order to destroy the political power of the capitalists and to establish their own power?" And I went on to say:

"In countries, such as Germany and Italy, where the fascists have destroyed every right that the workers ever had, it is perfectly clear that the workers will be compelled to use violence in order to get rid of their fascist oppressors. But how

59

about the United States, England or France?" – the pamphlet was written in 1938 before the Vichy government took control – "In these countries the workers have the right to vote. Why is it not possible for them to elect a majority of socialists in Congress or in Parliament and establish socialism by law?"

"A peaceful change," I wrote, "is an ideal most desirable. Everyone, especially the revolutionary socialists, will subscribe to that idea" – I say a peaceful change, I do not say a violent one.

"The question, however, is not whether it is desirable but whether it is possible. On the statute books of most of the states there are 'criminal syndicalism' laws" – and the Smith Law, upon which the second count of this indictment is based, is a criminal syndicalism law – "providing long prison sentences for anyone who advocates the overthrow of the government by violence. Such laws will be as effective as laws against the occurrence of earthquakes. For revolutions cannot be prevented by any law. Like convulsions in nature, they are the result of the evolution of forces beyond the power of man to stop."

Then here comes the significant section, the section that should settle all doubts concerning the question –

"On the basis of history and of theory, we are justified in predicting that the capitalist class will not surrender power to the working class without a violent struggle. History knows no example of the peaceful surrender of an exploiting minority to an oppressed majority. The actual conduct of the capitalist class at the present time, the violence which it uses against the workers when they strike for an improvement in their conditions, confirm the historical lesson, and justify the prediction that they, who will lose their wealth and power, will utilize all forms of violence against the overwhelming majority."

What possible interpretation can anyone who is free of

prejudice place upon that paragraph other than that I predict, but I do not advocate the use of violence. I concluded:

"The form of government in the United States practically guarantees the ruling class its domination against the will of the majority of the people. To introduce socialism by law would require an amendment to the Constitution and for that, a two-thirds majority of both houses of Congress and a majority in three-fourths of the state legislatures are required. Thirteen small and backward states could prevent any amendment to the Constitution. Revolutionary socialists all favor a peaceful transformation of the present order to the socialist order" – we favor it, we want it, we desire it, then how, I ask, can we advocate the contrary – "but he is insane who thinks that millions of workers will consent to starve because a minority of exploiters will threaten to, and will actually use violence against them."

I continue reading:

"If there is any one thing that will prevent the capitalists from using violence, it will be the strong organizations of the working class. The greater the strength of the working class organizations, the less violence will there be."

If, after reading this section of my pamphlet and after reading my column published in **The Militant** of March 29, 1941, the prosecution still insists on pressing this case, it must be that Washington wants a conviction regardless of the evidence. Possibly the prosecution missed this section of my pamphlet and missed the column which I wrote, but they know about them now and have known about them for several weeks; and for the prosecution to continue this case can mean nothing else but a determination to get a conviction regardless of the evidence.

If you consider what motives have led the defendants into the socialist movement you can realize how absurd it is to

61

accuse them of advocating violence. You have seen enough of the defendants and heard enough about their theories to convince you, I am certain, that it was not for personal gain that the defendants have become socialists. We are in a small minority and can therefore expect for a long time to come to meet only with hatred and scoffing, with persecution and prosecution. You can realize that we are in the socialist movement because we are devoted to its ideas and ideals.

If there is any one thing that impelled us to join the socialist movement, it is a hatred of the violence that exists in society – not only the physical violence but spiritual and moral violence – the violence which condemns children to starvation or semi-starvation because of the poverty of the parents, the violence which condemns children to go to work long before they have received an adequate education. Everywhere in society there is violence of one sort or another, culminating in the dreadful violence which sacrifices millions of human beings upon the altar of war. It is this violence which we hate that drives us into a movement which has as its ideal the creation of a world free from violence, where human beings will cooperate in the production of goods to satisfy their needs, where peace and security will prevail.

We are, of course, not pacifists. We do not believe with Gandhi that it is wrong for three hundred million people in India to use violence to drive out the British oppressors who claim to be fighting a war for democracy. As much as we hate the violence that exists in society, we see no alternative to the necessity of destroying the violence of the minority with the violence of the majority. But to accuse us of wanting and advocating violence is to accuse us of something that is revolting to our very nature.

Perhaps it would be fitting to close this section of my argument by quoting some people who are not in the ranks of the defendants and who can hardly be accused of being against the government.

"This country, with its institutions, belongs to the people who inhabit it. Whenever they shall grow weary of the existing government, they can exercise their constitutional right of amending it, or their revolutionary right to dismember or overthrow it."

None other than Abraham Lincoln said this, in his first inaugural address.

"I hold a little revolution now and then as necessary in the political world as storms in the physical."

The man who uttered this sentiment is not on trial. It was Thomas Jefferson.

Our Position on the War

It would stand to reason that, once having settled the central question of the case, whether or not we advocate or predict violence, there should not be much more to say. But you will excuse me, ladies and gentlemen, if I continue the argument on matters that in my opinion are subsidiary but which the prosecution has emphasized over and over again. There is always the danger that Mr. Anderson will claim that something is undenied and uncontradicted and perhaps it will be said, if I refrain from discussing other matters in the case, that I was afraid to do so.

The government follows a simple principle. It first assumes that the defendants are guilty of conspiring to advocate the overthrow of the government by force and violence and then it introduces evidence of our position and policies on various questions in order to prove that all of our activities are based on one motive and that is to further the conspiracy. If the defendants oppose the war, that shows that they are guilty of the central conspiracy; if they are active in the trade unions, that

63

proves the same thing, and thus with all the activities of the defendants.

There are many people in this country who oppose our entry into the war, but since they are not members of the Socialist Workers Party they have the right to do so, but we who are members of the Socialist Workers Party have no such right.

The government of course did not have to introduce any evidence with reference to our opposition to the war; we would gladly have stipulated that we are guilty of that. As a matter of fact, the government could have shortened the case by at least two weeks if it had come to us and asked us to admit the facts on a great many questions which it laboriously attempted to prove. We could have stipulated that we oppose the war, that we visited Leon Trotsky and that we sent men to guard him, that we advocate the creation of workers' defense guards, etc. These things are found in our writings. Ninety per cent of what the government tried to prove, we would have stipulated to and we could then have gone to the heart of the question as to whether or not we conspired to advocate the overthrow of the government by force. But since the government took all this trouble to prove things that we admit, it is necessary for me to explain those policies and analyze them.

The government accuses us of two things with reference to the war: one, that we oppose it, and two, that we intend to take advantage of a revolutionary situation which we expect the war to create.

While it is true that we hold wars to be inevitable under the capitalist system, it is also true that we would like to avoid them. War is the greatest destructive force in modern society. If this war should last for years, it may well be that all the resources of society will be exhausted and not even a social revolution could solve the problems of mankind. With the exhaustion of all the material and spiritual forces of society, the possibility of creating a new social system is very slim. We would then have to wait until the material and spiritual resources of mankind are resuscitated.

It is our duty to prevent war if possible and to shorten the war if war is declared in spite of our efforts. We shall try to convince the masses that in order to live and in order to permit their children and their children's children to live, they are under an obligation to end the war and create a socialist order.

There is at present no law making it a crime to oppose the war. But I am safe in saying that our opposition to the war is one of the most important, if not the most important, factors in explaining this prosecution. The rules of evidence do not permit us, as I indicated before, to go into the motives for the prosecution; but I would say that the address of Mr. Anderson yesterday and the emphasis which the prosecution has placed throughout the course of the trial on the party's position with reference to the war and with reference to our policy on military training, justifies the conclusion that to a large extent it is our opposition to the war that explains this prosecution.

To justify the introduction of our position on the war into evidence, the government contends that our opposition to the entry of the United States into the war, and our statement that we will continue to oppose the war even after the United States declares war, are evidence that we are conspiring to overthrow the government by force and violence. A far-fetched and an unreasonable contention! There are pacifists, conscientious objectors and others opposed to the war who are not interested in establishing socialism or overthrowing the government. There are socialists of a type that support the war. Only we revolutionary socialists who oppose the war are prosecuted.

As I indicated, there is no law preventing us from opposing the war. Nor is there a law which prohibits people from saying that they will continue to oppose the war even after war is declared. Of course when war is declared, the Espionage

Act will come into effect, making certain statements about the war unlawful, but thus far war has not been declared and I am certain that no one could be convicted simply for a statement that he intends to oppose the war even after it is declared.

We Oppose Imperialist Wars

Our reasons for our opposition to the war have been sufficiently clarified by the testimony of the defense and I need not go into detail. We consider the war on the part of England, of Germany, of France, of Italy, of Japan and of the United States as imperialist in character. We do not hesitate to admit that. We have written and said it thousands of times.

What do we mean by characterizing the war on the part of these countries as imperialist? 'We mean that the ruling classes which are responsible for the war and which lead the masses into the war are fighting to protect or to acquire markets, colonies, sources of raw material and spheres of influence. Germany wants the colonies that England has, England came upon the scene first, grabbed off most of the rich colonies in the world, and now Germany is trying to get some of these colonies away from England. The United States has not very many colonies in the strict sense of the word, but it has billions of dollars invested in Latin America and in other parts of the world and it wants markets in China, in the Far East.

One of the government witnesses, Mr. Harris I believe, was a member of the Marine Corps and he testified that he was stationed in China some time ago and Mr. Anderson praised him to the sky for serving his country in China. We do not conceal our belief that the marines in China are not there to protect the interests of the people of the United States but the interests of the Standard Oil Company and other big companies who have investments in China. The capitalists of this country are not interested in the development of China; they are interested in China because it furnishes them a market for the sale of their goods and a field for the investment of their capital.

The same thing is true with reference to Latin America. Roosevelt, representing the interests of the American capitalists, is not interested in the welfare of the people of Latin America. The claim that the present administration is interested in fighting for democracy can be disproved by the fact that when Franco was fighting the Loyalist government in Spain, the present administration declared its neutrality. It was not interested in defending democracy so long as there was no threat to the economic interests of the American capitalist class.

When we state that this is an imperialist war, it follows that we cannot possibly support the administration in its war efforts. You may not agree with us – some of you undoubtedly think that we are wrong – but I hope that in considering the evidence in this case, your opinion as to the correctness or incorrectness of our attitude on the war will not sway in the least your decision.

Mr. Cannon explained in his testimony for the defense that opposition to the war means non-support in a political sense. If any member of our party were a member of Congress, he would not vote for a declaration of war, nor would he vote for the war budget. No matter how much we may antagonize any jury, we must say that because it is the truth.

Certain expressions found in some of the literature introduced by the government have been emphasized by the prosecution, especially the expression, "Turn imperialist war into civil war." This expression is not found in our **Declaration of Principles**. I never used it either in my pamphlet or in any of the columns I wrote for **The Militant**. But it has been used, and by great socialists, and at times it has been repeated by some of our members. If you should take this expression into consideration, you must take it in connection with our general program which says that we must win over a majority of the people. The expression is correctly interpreted as follows: If, in the midst of the war or at the end of the war, a majority of the people, tired and weary and driven by the agony and suffering to which they will be subjected by the war, accept our ideas and decide to take power, then if the minority resists, the result will be that the imperialist war will be turned into a civil war. That is the only correct way to interpret that expression in the light of our **Declaration of Principles** which says that we must win a majority of the people over to our ideas.

We say now and we shall continue to say it as long as we are permitted, that war is a result of the conflict between imperialist nations.

The exhibits introduced by the government show that long before the war began we predicted that it would come. Were we then responsible for it when we predicted its coming? Who is responsible for the war? In the last analysis, not even Hitler, who fired the first shot, is responsible. As far as we are concerned, the responsibility for this war is primarily upon the system that creates the imperialist rivalries. On the basis of the present system, Leagues of Nations, Kellogg Peace Pacts and all the good intentions in the world cannot preserve peace.

Most of you are old enough to remember the statements that were made during the last war, that it was a war for democracy and it was a war to end wars. And the results of the last war are visible to everyone – fascism and now another war. Who was right? Socialists like Lenin who said that without socialist revolutions all over the world there will be more imperialist wars, or the people who proclaimed that the First World War was the last war? We can predict with absolute certainty the same thing that Lenin predicted in the First World War: if socialism does not come, more wars will follow.

Fascism Must Be Destroyed – How?

The vast majority of the people of this country are

terribly afraid of Hitler and justifiably so. I don't think the isolationists are correct when they say that we do not have to fear an invasion of this country by Hitler. It is not a question of invasion; it is a question of imperialist rivalries and Hitler is no doubt the greatest potential enemy of the ruling group in this country and above all he is the greatest potential enemy of the American masses. The destruction of Hitler – and I am using Hitler as a symbol of fascism – is a task which should be undertaken by everyone who values freedom and culture. No nation is sure of liberty so long as fascism exists anywhere in the world.

But the question is: What method should be used in exterminating the fascist danger? We contend that this war is not a war against Hitlerism. The British ruling class is not hostile to fascism. It can be taken as an elementary proposition that the British ruling class is not interested in preserving democracy.

The people of Great Britain and the people of this country are interested in democracy and want to fight for it, but in our opinion to fight under the leadership of the Churchill government or under the leadership of any other capitalist government is to fight not for democracy but for the financiers and industrialists.

Even assuming that Hitler should be defeated, fascism will not be destroyed because fascism is not a product of Hitler but it is a product of a decaying capitalist system. Dislocation of economy is bound to follow this war; millions of men will be thrown out of work, misery and suffering will be their lot and in such a situation fascism is bound to flourish. It is in such a situation that the fascist demagogues of Germany succeeded in gaining power. The German people, crushed and humiliated by the Versailles peace, not given a chance to work and live, were thrown into the arms of Hitler. Should capitalism continue to exist after this war, fascism is inevitable unless the masses of people take their fate into their own hands and create a socialist order.

Should war last a long time, the possibility of a peace between the rival imperialist nations is very great. The British ruling class and the American ruling class can easily come to terms with Hitler if they cannot defeat him, but not so the working masses; they must fight Hitler to the very death – especially the socialists who know the fate that awaits them if Hitler is victorious.

The prosecution's statement that in a war between the United States and Germany the defendants will prefer a victory of Germany is made either because of complete ignorance of our position or because of a malicious intention to falsify our position. Mr. Anderson said that in his opening statement. At that time, he did not perhaps know our position with reference to this question. Let no one dare, however, to stand up before you now after the exhibits have been introduced and say that we want a Hitler victory.

Our Program to Defeat Fascism

We say that to defeat Hitlerism it is necessary for the masses to assume leadership in that struggle.

What is the fundamental reason for Hitler's victories? Is it simply because he has been preparing for a longer time? How could he win his victories if a large section of the German people did not support him? To say that the German people, a great and cultured people, willingly accept the violent regime of Hitler is to insult the Germans. They are, however, given no alternative; it is either supporting Hitler or suffering a crushing defeat at the hands of the British imperialists and they fear that more than they fear a Hitler victory.

Hitler can come to the German people and say truthfully: The British ruling class has a monopoly on the wealth of this world; we ought to have our share of it. When he attacks Churchill and the British ruling class, he is speaking the truth – at least 90 per cent of the time; when he talks about his own intentions, he speaks nothing but lies. The same is true of Churchill who tells the truth only when he is attacking Hitler.

The situation would be entirely changed if in England the workers would establish their own socialist government and if in the United States a workers' and farmers' government would displace the present capitalist government.

Socialist governments in England and the United States would proclaim to the German people: "We have nothing against you; all we want is that you join us in creating a cooperative commonwealth throughout the whole world. We have no ambitions against your territory and we shall not do anything to deprive you of your liberty; revolt against Hitler and establish your own socialist government." Hitler could not last one week after such an appeal. He would be destroyed by his own people.

This is our solution to the problem of Hitlerism. Unfortunately we are as yet too small a group really to influence the thought of the masses. It is not we who will create difficulties for the ruling class in this country; it is the war that will create those difficulties. Let us assume a war which will last five or even more years; the cost of living will be going up; over 50 per cent of our productive efforts will go for war purposes; the people in this country will be suffering as well as the people in England and in Germany and in Italy; and we hope that the day will come when all the peoples of the various countries will fraternize and put an end to the conflict which is now being fought to guard the interests of the ruling cliques.

It is nonsense to think that a small party like ours can, by its agitation, create dissatisfaction. 'What creates dissatisfaction is the war and we are not responsible for that.

71

The class struggle goes on during the war whether we agitate for it or not. We have very little influence in the labor movement but the struggle goes on right now. With the cost of living going up, the workers are bound to strike for higher wages and he is indeed foolish who thinks that, when we are behind bars, strikes will cease. Neither will a revolutionary situation be prevented by putting us behind bars. It would be necessary to put the whole working class behind bars in order to assure the capitalists the kind of peace that they want. Hitler thinks that by his methods of force he can bring to an end the class struggle and this trial is an indication that the same methods will be used in this country. The specter of fascism haunts this trial – a mass trial that is characteristic of trials in Italy and in Germany.

I do not mean to say that fascism is here; we still have a chance to argue before a jury, but the very fact that a large number of people can be dragged into court because of their ideas and writings is an indication that the monster of fascism is coming ever closer to us.

"Revolutionary defeatism" is another expression that the prosecution points to as something terrible to contemplate. I expressly defined that phrase in the column that I referred to before, published in **The Militant** of March 29, 1941. It simply means that we continue to advocate the class struggle during the war. By that is meant that if the workers have any grievances, they should demand the settlement of those grievances and if no settlement is made, they should go on strike. Will that interfere with the military effort? The responsibility is not that of the workers but of the employers who refuse to settle the grievances.

What Political Opposition Means

In that same article I state that we want to carry on our agitation and gain a majority even during the war. But so long

72

as we have no majority, there is nothing for us to do except to submit to the majority. "To submit to the majority," ladies and gentlemen, that phrase is found several times in my column. Do the prosecutors expect us to change our ideas because there is a war? Do they want us to stop thinking? Yes, we want to convince workers and soldiers that our ideas are correct and until we convince the majority, we are willing to submit to the decisions of the majority. For any government to demand anything more than that means practically introducing fascism.

In that article I expressly state that our party opposes sabotage, opposes any individual or group action which would obstruct the conduct of the war. If the prosecutors were fair and had the power to dismiss this case, they would do so without hesitation the moment their attention was brought to this column. He who would contend, after reading that article, that we are in favor of a victory of Hitler or that we would practice sabotage, does not want to read correctly.

Of course, under Mr. Anderson's theory, to teach socialism constitutes, in and of itself, sabotage. He stated that, but he does not claim that we would try to sabotage the army by doing something to the rifles or to the planes or cannons so that they could not be used properly. The prosecutors simply claim that, if the soldiers listen to our theories, they will not fight for the government. In other words, socialism is sabotage to the prosecutors regardless of the fact that we say over and over again that so long as we are not in a majority, we can do nothing but what we are told to do.

The Court: We will adjourn now.

Friday, November 28, 1941
Morning Session

The Court: You may proceed.

Mr. Goldman: Once more I beg your indulgence for taking so much of your time. Last night I went through my notes and I cut out enough to shorten my argument by about four hours. If, in your deliberations, someone asks why did not Goldman touch upon this matter and that matter, then the answer is that I had to refrain from discussing many questions because of lack of time.

Yesterday, in discussing the question of whether or not we advocate or predict violence, I forgot to mention the fact that in the majority of instances where violence is mentioned in the exhibits, it refers to defense against the fascists. This is an important point which I ask you to consider in your deliberations.

Our Military Policy

The indictment charges us with conspiring to create insurrection and disobedience in the armed forces of the United States. It is important to discuss our so-called military policy. The government depends upon that policy, I think, in its attempt to convince you that we are guilty of that section of the indictment.

When the question of compulsory military service was first taken up in Congress and a discussion upon it began in the country, our party felt it necessary to take a position on that question.

As you know, there are people in this country who are

pacifists and conscientious objectors who, under no circumstances, would fight in the armed forces or even allow themselves to be drafted for military service. There are many socialists who take a similar stand.

We, on the other hand, considered the situation from its fundamental aspect, namely, that in this epoch when fascism has come upon the scene with its horrible violence, it is futile not to recognize the fact that all important questions will be settled by military means. Not only futile, but extremely dangerous! Of all groups in society, we are most vehemently opposed to war but so long as war exists in the world and so long as there are fascists ready to use violence against the working class, every worker has the duty of training to defend himself. Young people will have to go to war whether they like it or not and since that is the case, we are in favor of having our youth trained in the arts of war. Modern warfare requires great technical skill and he is foolish who does not understand that it is necessary to acquire that skill.

We cannot tell the young generation to oppose military training when we know that it will be dragged into war. And it is on the basis of this fundamental proposition that we say to the young men: Do not resist compulsory military training; go into the army and do your best to get the training necessary to defend yourselves against the enemy from without and – we also added – against the enemy from within. In a world where fascism and violence and war dominate the scene, it is necessary for you to accept military training in order to defend yourselves.

Naturally, we would like our members, wherever they are, in the factory or in a union or in the army, to propagate our ideas, but we understand that the army is not a place where one can speak as freely as outside of the army. We don't like it but we are realistic enough to understand that in the army it is necessary to be cautious. Just as a trade unionist in an open shop must be careful in propagating his ideas for trade unionism, so must a soldier in the army be careful in propagating ideas frowned upon by the generals. In the army, of course, it is far more dangerous to propagate socialism than it is to propagate trade unionism in an open shop. The greatest open shop institution in this country is the United States Army.

Conditions in our army are not so bad now as they were fifty or a hundred years ago. There was a time when it was impossible for a human being who was not brutalized to remain in the army. That has been changed and not without a struggle.

At present we advocate the idea that soldiers in the army should be on terms of equality with the officers. We consider the private soldiers equal in every way, except from the point of view of technical training, to the officers and we insist that they be treated in the same way as officers are treated. We advocate legislation compelling the officers to treat privates with respect and to change the rules which permit officers in charge of a military tribunal to inflict inhuman punishment for some minor infraction of the Military Code.

The government has introduced evidence that we urge the soldiers to kick about their food. I do not know whether there have been complaints about food in the army. If the food is not good, then the soldiers, including members of our party who are drafted, should kick about the food. If the prosecution is interested in preventing such complaints about the food, then let it see to it that the soldiers are provided with good food. Are we in a situation where soldiers must eat rotten food without complaining? That seems to be the theory of the prosecution.

Here I want to point out to you the absurdity of the accusation levelled against us to the effect that we send our members into the army in order to kick about food and create insubordination. Do you think we could win any influence in that way, and after all, that is our main aim – to win people over to our ideas, and thus gain influence. How do you think Vincent

Dunne and Farrell Dobbs and Miles Dunne and Carl Skoglund and all the other leaders of Local 544 succeeded in gaining influence over the truck drivers? Simply by kicking?

And certainly not by proclaiming themselves to be Trotskyists. You can readily assume that the 6,000 truck drivers do not follow their leadership because it is composed of Socialist Workers Party members. The vast majority of the truck drivers is composed of Republicans, Democrats and Farmer-Laborites. But these people also voted for Farrell Dobbs and Vincent and Miles Dunne as their union leaders. Why? Because they saw in them men who have served their interests. The truck drivers may not even like the fact that those defendants who are leaders of Local 544 are socialists; but still they vote for them because they see in the defendants men who guard the interests of the workers. Our party members in Local 5-11 did not win influence among the truck drivers because they taught socialism, but because they improved the conditions under which the truck drivers worked.

The same thing holds with reference to any of our members who may be in the army. They cannot gain influence by teaching the abstract doctrine of socialism, but by taking care of the soldiers' interests. It is true that we take advantage of every opportunity to teach the ideas of socialism. But we feel the socialist ideas will take root, not at present, when the vast majority of the people is satisfied with its conditions, but in the future when the masses will be driven to accept new ideas because of their suffering and privations. Human beings are very slow to change their ideas. The human mind is surrounded by a crust of all the ideas it has absorbed from childhood, and not until events destroy that crust is it ready to accept new ideas. It is because we want to get the confidence of the workers and the soldiers that we defend their immediate interests, and do not merely teach them the abstract doctrine of socialism.

We have put forth the idea of military training under

trade union control. As Mr. Cannon testified, a training camp was operated in Plattsburg, New York, for the purpose of training business men and professional men as officers, and the government furnished the necessary funds. Why not have training camps where trade unions could train their men both as soldiers and as officers?

In our opinion the great majority of generals and higher officers in the army are hostile to the laboring class. The higher officers are raised and trained in an environment which makes them hostile to the workers. They are not interested in democracy or in fighting for democracy. Have not the events in France confirmed our opinion in that respect? The American and British generals are not any different from the French generals. Who surrendered to Germany? Not the rank and file, but Petain and Weygand and the other generals in command of the French army. Who permitted the Germans to enter Norway? Not the rank and file soldiers, but the fascists in the upper ranks. We say plainly that we do not trust the generals and higher officers to fight for democracy.

Because of that we propose that the trade unions train their own officers – officers in whom the workers can have confidence and whom they can control. And you must remember, when you consider this point, that the trade unions are not under the control of the Socialist Workers Party, but under the control of men who are, from our viewpoint, very conservative, and even reactionary. Still, rather than have officers trained at West Point, we prefer to have them trained under trade union control because the trade unions are organizations of workers. Furthermore, you must remember that our program of military training under trade union control is a legislative program. We want Congress to pass legislation making such training possible by appropriating funds for that purpose.

Of course, as with all other activities and policies of the

Socialist Workers Party, our idea of military training under trade union control is evidence, as far as the prosecution is concerned, of a conspiracy to overthrow the government by force. No matter what we do, it is taken by the government as evidence of this conspiracy. If we opposed military training, that would constitute evidence of a conspiracy; when we are for military training, that is brought in as evidence of a conspiracy!

Why We Want Workers' Defense Guards

Another policy of ours which the government introduced as evidence of a conspiracy is our proposal of establishing workers' defense guards. We have no hesitation to admit that we would like to see the workers create such defense guards. I shall even admit – and let the government make the most of it – that if workers' defense guards should be created, they would defend the revolution of the majority against the violence of the minority. We shall do our utmost to create workers' defense guards so that when the majority of the people take power, it will be able to put down any revolt by the minority.

The charge that is levelled against us, you must remember, is that we are conspiring to overthrow and to advocate the overthrow of the government by force and violence. The government must first prove that charge beyond a reasonable doubt, and it cannot prove it by introducing evidence that we advise the establishment of workers' defense guards or a union defense guard. If the jury agrees with me that we do not advocate the use of violence, but predict that the minority will use violence against the majority, then everything else is immaterial. It is perfectly proper for us to propose to workers the idea of creating defense guards to protect them against fascist violence, and mind you, we are not advocating a policy of creating defense guards of our own members. We want the workers to build these defense guards.

80

Unfortunately, they have not as yet followed our proposals. The fascist danger is not so evident to the workers as it is to us, and they have not acted in accordance with our proposals. This is a fine example of the idea that it is not agitation that can bring certain things into existence. If conditions are not ripe for it, then we can talk from now until doomsday and the workers will not follow our advice. There is not a single workers' defense guard in the United States today.

Mr. Schweinhaut (Prosecutor): That statement, that there is not a single defense guard in the United States today, is not brought out by the evidence. The contrary has been established. As a matter of fact, in March of this year the Union Defense Guard was in existence in Minneapolis.

Mr. Goldman: I still contend on the basis of the evidence that there does not exist a single defense guard in the United States at the present time.

The Court: Well, the jury will remember what the evidence was on that particular question.

544 Defense Guard

I shall now deal with the question of the Union Defense Guard of Local 544. What relationship did the existence of this Union Defense Guard of the Minneapolis truck drivers have to our proposal for a workers' defense guard? The idea of a workers' defense guard, as has been explained to you, is not something new. It has not only been propagated by us, but we have actually, on certain occasions, created a defense guard to defend our meetings against Stalinist and fascist hoodlums. As a matter of fact, there have been defense guards ever since the socialist movement began, because there have always been elements who wanted to use violence against socialists.

And when a situation arose in Minneapolis which demanded the formation of some kind of defense organization

81

to defend the right of union men to hold their meetings undisturbed and to protect the halls and property of the union, our members, trained in the idea of having defense guards, naturally thought of creating such a guard to protect the interests of Local 544.

Members of our party are superior to the average worker, if they are superior at all, because they have a certain theory as to the basis of their activities, and this theory enables them to predict and act upon their predictions. The average worker lives from day to day – he works, earns his living, is thrown out of his job, goes on relief, has children and tries to feed them. He is unable as yet to generalize the reasons for his difficulties. A member of the Socialist Workers Party thinks in general terms about the situation of the workers in society. He is trained to understand that his life is bound up with the life of his class.

As I said, we have a theory of society, and on the basis of that theory we are able to predict that certain people will act in a certain way. We know, for instance, that the fascists will at one time or another make an attempt to destroy the unions. When our members saw in the Minneapolis newspapers in 1938 reports that the Silver Shirts were organizing, they also understood that the Silver Shirts were not organizing to benefit the trade unions, but to destroy them. Our members immediately considered what to do to defend the union hall, the union property and the union meetings against the attacks of the Silver Shirts. Whereas the average worker does not think of the future, our members do.

Yesterday, in his argument, Mr. Anderson made a very peculiar remark. "What business," he asked, "is it of theirs to bring the history of the Russian revolution into the United States?" I am sorry that Mr. Anderson is puzzled by that, but our party members are taught to study everything that happens in the world. What happens in Russia, in England, in Africa, is our business. We do not believe that the United States can be separated from the rest of the world. It is part of the world, and whatever happens in any section of the world affects us. We studied what the fascists did in Germany and in Italy, and because we studied the activities of the fascists there, we know what the activities of the American fascists will be here. And we teach the workers not to wait until the fascists succeed here, as they succeeded in Germany and Italy. We teach workers to organize their workers' defense guards and prevent the fascists from doing here what they did in other countries.

Why did Local 544 and not any other union in Minneapolis organize a union defense guard? Everyone knows that Local 544 is the most important union in Minneapolis. It was considered the arch-enemy of the reactionary employers and of the fascists, and everyone with any common sense understood that when fascists were organizing in Minneapolis, they would attack 544 first of all. Our members understood that and that is why Local 544 took the initiative and organized the Union Defense Guard. But it must be remembered that they invited the members of other unions to participate in this defense guard.

The Undisputed Fact About the Guard

The government witnesses practically proved everything we wanted to prove to the jury on the question of the Union Defense Guard. The evidence on that question was the greatest dud that the government produced. I am only amazed that the prosecutors still insist on injecting the question of the Union Defense Guard into this case. Were they really fair-minded, they would openly state to the jury that the Union Defense Guard is not to be considered by the jury as evidence against the defendants. Their failure to do so is another indication to me that the prosecutors are unable to act independently in this case, and must follow orders of people higher up.

By the testimony of the government witnesses it has been proved that the Union Defense Guard was organized at the time the Silver Shirts became active in Minneapolis late in the summer of 1938. Our evidence that the Minneapolis newspapers carried news items describing the activities of the Silver Shirts has not and cannot be denied. All the government witnesses, with the exception of one, testified that at the Union Defense Guard meetings Vincent Dunne and other defendants explained the necessity of organizing the Guard against the possible attacks of the Silver Shirts.

The only one who testified that Vincent Dunne told 150 members of the Union Defense Guard that the purpose of the organization was to overthrow the government was Elmer Buckingham. If you remember that witness, you remember that he was slouching and constantly looking at the floor. He testified that he did not remember anything about the Silver Shirts, but that he remembered Vincent Dunne, in the presence of about 150 men, state that the purpose of the Defense Guard was to overthrow the government of the United States.

All I ask is that the jurors ask themselves one question: Is it credible that Vincent Dunne, an intelligent individual, if he actually organized the Union Defense Guard to overthrow the government, would state his purpose at an open meeting in the presence of 150 men? When one takes that factor into consideration and in addition remembers that no other government witness heard Vincent Dunne say anything of the kind, then it becomes clear how much credence can be placed in the testimony of Buckingham.

It is not denied by us that the Union Defense Guard had target practice. One government witness testified that target practice was decided upon as a form of entertainment. I do not even deny that there is a possibility that the members of the Guard wanted target practice with the idea in mind of training the members to shoot so that they could defend themselves

84

against any armed attack. They had a perfect right to have target practice even if the intention was to learn how to shoot so that they could defend themselves against any armed attack.

Was the Guard Necessary?

Mr. Anderson asks why the leaders of Local 544 did not ask the government authorities for protection. Why was it necessary to organize the Guard? In the first place, even if a person notifies the authorities and asks for protection against a possible attack, he is not thereby prevented from preparing to defend himself. Local 544 could have notified the authorities and then proceeded to organize a union defense guard. There was no attempt to conceal the fact that a union defense guard was organized. The organization met openly. Many people in Minneapolis knew about the existence of the Guard. The **Northwest Organizer,** official organ of all the Minneapolis Teamsters unions, was full of news about it. And there can be no question but that the police knew about it.

Indeed the leaders of Local 544 did not have very great confidence in the authorities and did not rely upon them very greatly for protection against the Silver Shirts. It is evident to everyone that neither the city, nor the state, nor the federal government was favorably inclined to Local 544. Under such conditions the leaders of Local 544 would have been derelict in their duty had they not taken steps to organize a guard to protect the members and their union.

That the Guard was organized, not for the purpose of overthrowing the government but to defend the union against the Silver Shirts, is proved conclusively by the fact that it was organized when first the Silver Shirts came to Minneapolis, and that it ceased to exist as a functioning organization in the spring of 1939 when the Silver Shirts no longer held meetings in Minneapolis. After 1939 the Union Defense Guard was called together only for the purpose of policing picnics or Christmas parties. Only the prosecuting attorneys can draw from that fact the conclusion that the Union Defense Guard still exists as a functioning guard organization.

Undoubtedly the members of our party in Local 544 took the initiative in organizing the Union Defense Guard. They prepared for any eventuality; and the fact that the Silver Shirts did not attack does not prove Mr. Anderson's point that the Union Defense Guard was not organized to defend the union against the Silver Shirts, but simply proves that "an ounce of preparation is worth a pound of cure." As a result of the readiness of the members of Local 544 to defend themselves, the Silver Shirts did not dare launch any attack.

The Union Defense Guard, the one issue which the government announced with great fanfare before the trial as indicating that there was a real conspiracy to overthrow the government by force, has been completely shattered, and by the government's own witnesses. That the government has not honestly and frankly admitted its mistake is an indication, as I said before, that in this case the government wants a conviction regardless of the evidence.

Lessons of Russian Revolution

The prosecution was very anxious to prove two things about the Russian revolution – one, that we consider it a great event and were consequently interested in it and, two, that we studied it in order to imitate here the tactics that were used by the Bolshevik Party under the leadership of Lenin and Trotsky.

I simply want to emphasize the one fact that should by this time be clear, even to the prosecution. The Russian revolution was not the result of a conspiracy organized by a minority. It was the work of the immense majority of the workers and peasants supporting the Bolshevik Party led by Lenin and Trotsky.

Conclusive evidence of the fact that the vast majority of the people of Russia supported the Bolshevik Party is the successful struggle of the Red Army, organized by Leon Trotsky, against a powerful combination of forces consisting of Russian White Guards, the Czecho-Slovak army, Japanese, English and even American soldiers. Had the Bolshevik Party not been supported by 95 per cent of the Russian people, it could never have withstood such a powerful attack.

The second lesson to be drawn from the Russian revolution, as far as this case is concerned, is that it was a minority of capitalists and landlords who began the civil war in order to prevent the majority from trying to establish the foundations of a new social order.

For us, the Russian revolution is all-important because for the first time in history the masses of people actually took the productive wealth away from the capitalists and landlords. The foundations of socialism were created by the Russian revolution. Unfortunately, historic conditions, which I am unable to discuss because they are not germane to the case, permitted a bureaucratic clique under the leadership of Stalin to usurp power and to crush every form of democracy in the Soviet Union.

Mr. Anderson advises the defendants to go to Russia if we are so interested in that country. It should be known, even to Mr. Anderson, that Trotskyists have no chance at all to live in the Soviet Union; thousands of them have been executed. The best army and naval officers have been executed and this is why the Russian soldiers, in spite of the most heroic resistance, have sustained defeats at the hands of the Nazi army.

Mr. Schweinhaut: Is that evidence?

Mr. Goldman: No, that is not part of the evidence in this case. It may be disregarded by the jury. It is in evidence, however, that the Trotskyists in the Soviet Union struggled for democratic rights in that country just as we struggle for democratic rights here. Mr. Anderson should know that most of the defendants were born in this country and he above all should know that this country was built by so-called foreigners, by the Irish, the Swedes, the Russians, the Hungarians, the Italians, by the foreign workers who slaved in the mines, who built the railroads, who created the most powerful country in the world, now in the hands of the Sixty Families and their satellites. He should know that the Swedes and Norwegians were the ones who settled in Minnesota and helped build up this state. It is indeed a shame that people who were born here or who were raised here and who worked here should be told to get out of this country by the prosecution.

The defendants, of course, as I indicated yesterday, are internationalists. We make no distinctions between races and nationalities. Wherever we are, there we fight to the best of our abilities for liberty and democracy.

"History repeats itself" is a phrase that is frequently heard. But that is true to only a very limited extent. History actually never repeats itself. We do not know what the conditions will be under which the masses of this country decide to establish a socialist regime. We do know that they can never be exactly the same as existed in Russia in November 1917. Russia was largely an agricultural country with 80 per cent of the people illiterate, without any tradition of democracy. The farmers in the United States are not the same as the peasants of Russia. We have a right to hope that the higher standards of education in this country and the democratic traditions of the people will prevent the great tragedy that occurred in the Soviet Union subsequent to the revolution – I refer to the usurpation of power by the Stalinist clique that has crushed every form of democracy.

What did the prosecution succeed in doing by introducing our articles dealing with the Russian revolution?

Has it succeeded in proving a conspiracy on our part to overthrow the government by force and violence? It has succeeded only in proving that we, like the Bolsheviks in Russia, aim to win a majority of the people of this country to our ideas. If that is a "conspiracy," it will be a conspiracy of the vast majority of the people to change the present social order and to organize a government that will best protect their economic, political and social interests.

And should the minority attempt to use violence to thwart the will of the majority, then I hope that the masses will organize their workers' defense guard, just as the Russian workers organized their Red Army and just as the workers of 544 organized their Defense Guard to put down the violence of a minority.

It may be of some interest to note that this indictment was written subsequent to June 22, 1941, the date when Hitler invaded the Soviet Union. Since then there has been a very close and friendly relationship between the present administration and Stalin's government. It so happens that the former American ambassador to the Soviet Union, Mr. Davies, wrote an article recently in a popular magazine wherein he claims that the Trotskyists were fascists and that Stalin did well to have them executed. It is indeed peculiar that whereas Stalin accused the Trotskyists of being fascists, we here are accused of being revolutionists. Different governments have different ways of framing the Trotskyists.

Marx, Lenin and Trotsky

I did not know whether to laugh or to weep when Mr. Anderson, in his opening address, accused us of being Marxists. I was tempted to laugh because throughout this country in every institution of learning there are people teaching history, sociology, and even the physical sciences who consider themselves Marxists.

89

There are many people who claim to be Marxists. We may not agree that they are but at least they claim to be. And for Mr. Anderson to get up in a court of law in the United States and accuse people of being Marxists as if that were a crime is, to say the least, somewhat absurd.

But that accusation also had a very serious connotation. For it is in Germany and Italy that Marxism is considered a crime and where Marxists are exterminated.

I wonder if counsel for the government understood the full significance of their introduction into evidence of the **Communist Manifesto**. Their purpose in introducing the **Communist Manifesto** was, of course, to get the jury to convict the defendants. But that means practically banning a book which is being sold in every good bookstore in the United States, which is on the library shelves of every decent library, and which is studied in every university. For if we can be convicted for circulating the **Communist Manifesto** then, in effect, a ban is placed upon it. Hitler started the practice of burning books distasteful to him; and among the first books that he ordered burned were the books of Karl Marx and Frederick Engels, including the **Communist Manifesto**. I do not mean, Mr. Schweinhaut actually wants the **Communist Manifesto** burned but, in effect, by introducing the book into evidence, he condemns it and warns the world not to read or circulate it.

We, of course, must plead guilty to the charge of being Marxists. We are Marxists because we believe that the economic structure of society is the determining factor in social development and that man is a product of his social environment. We are Marxists because we believe that the productive forces of society have reached a stage where it is possible to produce everything necessary to satisfy the reasonable needs of the people; because we believe that capitalist society has reached a point when the people must either progress with socialism or perish through fascist

90

barbarism. In essence this is now the meaning of Marxism and to this charge we plead guilty.

Lenin as well as Marx was dragged into the case by the prosecution. And again we must admit that we consider Lenin as one of the great men of all times. His greatness lies in the fact that he was willing to stand alone with a few people supporting him in his opposition to the First World War when the vast majority of the socialists betrayed their principles and supported their own imperialist governments. Lenin in Switzerland and Trotsky in Vienna, in Paris and New York (he was expelled from Vienna and Paris during the war) both raised their voices against the First World War which they designated as imperialistic. Lenin predicted that the war would result in a revolutionary situation in Russia. His prediction came true and when that revolutionary situation actually came into existence, Lenin and Trotsky took advantage of it and led the masses in the revolution that destroyed capitalism in Russia.

The arch conspirator in this case, according to the government, is Leon Trotsky.

How absurd is the idea of designating Leon Trotsky as a conspirator! He has written three thick volumes on the history of the Russian revolution; he has written innumerable books and pamphlets explaining his ideas about society and current events. Critics have recognized his history of the Russian revolution as the greatest history penned by any man at any time. He is the type of man who, in addition to being a great theoretician and writer, could and did also organize and lead a great army.

We guarded his life because he meant so much to the movement that the defendants represent. Five or six secretaries gave their lives to guard him. We spent thousands of dollars in an effort to shield him from an attempt on his life that we were certain would some day be made by the Kremlin dictator. We do not deny that he was the one who guided our movement in its general aspects. Many of us visited him in Mexico many times.

91

We asked for his advice and he gave it to us, not on minor questions such as the organization of a union defense guard in Local 544, but on major questions of world importance. He discussed with us the role that the United States is playing and will play in world affairs. His analysis of events and his predictions on the basis of that analysis will always remain as evidence of his remarkable intellect. To call him a conspirator is an insult to human intelligence.

Yes, We Are Internationalists

The prosecution charges us with being internationalists and, of course, we must plead guilty to that charge. For us internationalism is the very heart of socialism. We conceive of the world as an economic unit. No nation, no matter how wealthy or powerful, can separate itself from the rest of the world. We are not isolationists. We do not believe that it is possible to isolate this country from the rest of the world.

As I indicated to you before, socialism is a world system under which all nations and all peoples will cooperate to produce enough goods to satisfy the reasonable needs of every human being. Every country will produce that which it is best fitted to produce. If a country can produce good machinery then let it not busy itself with producing agricultural products. Let some other country best fitted for the production of agricultural products produce those products and exchange its products for the machines produced by another country. Peace will come to a world cooperating in this way, which will be made possible only by socialism, which will do away with imperialist cliques fighting for colonies and markets.

We reject the idea that one nation or one people is superior to any other nation or any other people. To us all human beings are equal. The prejudices that exist are a product of the social system and not inherent in human nature. The brotherhood of man will be made possible and real under a socialist society which will do away with economic conflicts.

Our party belonged to the Fourth International. But when the Voorhis Act was enacted making it illegal for any organization in this country to belong to an international organization, we obeyed the law and severed our connection with the Fourth International. We did not like the law; we were opposed to it, but as a minority there was nothing for us to do except to obey it and try to have it repealed.

The Party and the Trade Unions

I come now to the question which I consider third in importance. First is the question of whether or not we advocate the violent overthrow of the government; second in importance is the question of our attitude on the war; and third is the question of our activities in the trade unions. When we consider that question we come to the point that actually explains the reason for this prosecution.

(Morning Recess)

Mr. Goldman: More time, ladies and gentlemen, was spent on the trade union question in this case than on any other single question, including the central issue of the case as to whether or not there is a conspiracy to overthrow the government by force and violence. And I am not surprised at that. I expected it because the trade union question has far more to do with this case than the question of the overthrow by force and violence of the government of the United States.

Consider the chief witnesses for the government – who they are, what they are doing now, what role they played in Local 544 before the indictment – and the conclusion is inescapable that this trial is essentially a contest between two factions in the union, with the government being part of one faction. I dare anyone to attempt to disprove that statement. Of course counsel for the government cannot admit that and they must try their best to disprove it. They must repeat over and over again: This case involves only the question of whether or not the defendants violated certain sections of the law. But all in vain! No matter what the government says, it cannot escape from the facts.

Therefore, I hope that you forgive me if I deal with the question of trade unionism, as it is involved in this case, quite extensively.

What did the government try to prove by introducing the question of trade unionism? It tried to prove that the Socialist Workers Party aims to gain control of the unions and to utilize that control for the purpose of getting the masses organized into unions to take up arms against the government. That in essence is the government's position.

Let us, then, analyze the evidence to see whether the government has succeeded in proving its contention. Mr. Anderson, in his opening statement, made it clear that the evidence would prove that the Socialist Workers Party conspired to dictate to the unions and to utilize the unions as instruments for the purpose of furthering the central aim of the party, to wit: to overthrow the government by force and violence. No other purpose was attributed by the prosecution to the Socialist Workers Party as far as the trade union question is concerned.

And then the parade of government witnesses began and on the basis of the testimony of those witnesses it could be deduced that the aim of the Socialist Workers Party in working within the unions was altogether different from that which Mr. Anderson indicated it was. Dictate to the unions! How could the Socialist Workers Party dictate to the unions of this country?

Even on the basis of the testimony of the government's own witnesses, as elicited from them through cross-examination, it became clear that the Socialist Workers Party never could and never did try to dictate to the unions. And when you take into consideration the evidence of the defendants, then you can see that all that the Socialist Workers Party aimed at was to have its members work in the unions, do the best they could for the workers and the unions and thus gain influence with the workers.

To work in the interest of the unions and thereby get the confidence of the workers and be elected to offices in the union, is a right which I shall defend day in and day out. Every person living in the United States, every group in this country, has a right to do exactly that. And as for us, we intend to exercise that right. It is unquestionably true, ladies and gentlemen, that the Socialist Workers Party would like to have great influence in the trade union movement so that it could persuade the workers to follow socialist ideas. Unfortunate for us and much to be regretted by us, is the fact that our influence in the trade union movement is very limited.

Every political party desires to get control of the unions. The question is for what purpose and in what manner? Can it be denied that the Democratic Party would like to get and retain control of the trade union movement? Can that be denied of the Republican Party or any other party? Of course not. Every political party attempts in various ways to get support in the trade union movement and as far as the Republican and Democratic Parties are concerned, they succeed in getting control of that movement through tying themselves up with the bureaucrats who lead that movement.

Our Faith in the Workers

The trade union movement is the most powerful institution in this country. Why? Because it includes in its ranks

95

vast numbers of industrial workers and railroad workers and is thus able to continue or to stop production and by stopping production, to throw the country into a terrific turmoil. If the trade union movement had leadership with social vision, it could easily solve the problems of this country but unfortunately the leadership is in the hands of narrow and bigoted men.

Our party supports the trade union movement against the employing class, even though certain sections of the unions are led by the type of men whom we designate as reactionary. We have so much faith in the essential correctness of the trade union movement – so much faith that the workers ultimately will throw the racketeers and bureaucrats off their backs – that we support the trade union organizations. As was said several times by government witnesses who did not understand the significance of their testimony, we are always in favor of the workers as a class, against the employers as a class. To us, the workers who create the wealth of society are always right against the employers who get the benefit of that work. That is why we support the workers against the employers even though the workers at times are led by people in whom we have no confidence whatever. It has been sufficiently brought out in the evidence that we do not have any confidence in Tobin, yet we would unhesitatingly support the Teamsters International, under the leadership of Tobin, against the employers.

The trade union movement at the present time, led by men like Tobin, who are interested only in their personal welfare, irritates many people. It irritates the small business men, the farmers and even many workers with the senseless jurisdictional struggles and clique fights constantly going on. As I said before, the leadership of the trade union movement lacks social vision and the task that we have set ourselves is to try to educate the members of the unions so that they will insist on having as their leaders men who understand the problems of society and who understand the power and the responsibility of the trade union movement in solving those problems.

Do we then attempt to control the trade union movement? If by that is meant that we send our members into the trade unions with instructions to work in the interest of the members of the trade unions and to gain the confidence of every worker and to be elected to office, then we must admit that we try to control it. But only in that sense and in no other sense. The history of Local 544 conclusively proves our contention that our work in the trade union movement is of that nature.

We are interested in bringing immediate benefits to the workers. Does it appear to be contradictory that socialists work to bring immediate benefits to the workers and at the same time look forward to a revolutionary situation when the masses will be dissatisfied with the dreadful conditions confronting them? Why is it that we try to improve the conditions of the workers? Remember that our object is to win the confidence of the masses and to do so we must work for an immediate improvement in their conditions. We must show them that their poverty and suffering are not brought about by anything they do, but by the existence of the capitalist system, by the greed of the capitalist class. We must show the workers that what we are interested in is improving their conditions.

But we also tell them that no matter how much we try to improve their immediate conditions, the social system under which they live makes it impossible in the long run to achieve any real improvement. Whether the workers like it or not, they will ultimately find themselves in a situation under the present social order when there will be no solution except to change that social order.

Our Record in Local 544

Under the strict rules of evidence it was impossible for

us to prove how much the defendants have done to improve the conditions under which the workers labor. But enough has been permitted into evidence to show beyond the peradventure of a doubt that the activities of the Dunne brothers, of Farrell Dobbs, of Cart Skoglund and of every other defendant who is a member of Local 544, aided the truck drivers in getting improved conditions. Can there be the slightest doubt of that? Who built Local 544? The defendants played by far the most important role in organizing the truck drivers. The evidence is overwhelming that in their activities the defendants were motivated by the fundamental aim of improving the conditions of the truck drivers and other workers and, what is more, they did succeed in improving the conditions of the workers in Minneapolis. You do not have to take our testimony for that, but the testimony of the witnesses for the government.

The defendants won the confidence of the truck drivers because we represented their interests. The truck drivers, who know nothing about socialism and surely nothing about Trotskyism, know the Dunnes, know Dobbs, know Skoglund and all the other defendants as people who are absolutely honest and sincere in their work. They know them personally and they understood that the defendants were working for the interests of the truck drivers.

Witness after witness for the government testified that they had been in opposition to the defendants, that they ran candidates against them in the elections of Local 544, but no one dared even to suggest that the defendants were not rightfully elected. The overwhelming testimony on the part of the government witnesses was to the effect that the defendants controlled Local 544 not by force, not by compulsion, but by virtue of winning the confidence of the men and of being elected to office in the most constitutional and democratic manner, with the rights of free speech and free criticism allowed to all opponents.

The membership of the truck drivers rose from 200 in 1934 to 6.500. Why do you think the truck drivers flocked into the union? Was it because the defendants were socialists or Trotskyists, or was it because the vast majority of them understood that they gained something practical by being in the union?

There were, of course, people like the government witnesses, who were not satisfied with Local 544 and its leadership. As I told you, modern society is constituted on the principle of "dog eat dog." There are many who try to benefit themselves at the expense of others and that is true of some people in the trade union movement. There is, in fact, no escaping from that principle anywhere under the present social system.

Two government witnesses came from Omaha. They turned out to be honest witnesses. These witnesses – Tommy Smith and Malcolm Love – testified that they joined the party not because they understood the principles of the party but because they knew Dobbs and they knew the Dunnes and, said Tommy Smith, because the leaders of Local 544 were "labor-minded"; they were "the only ones who helped other unions organize the unorganized." Dobbs went from one city to another helping his fellow workers and Tommy Smith said:

"I joined not because I knew anything about socialism but I knew the leaders of Local 544; I knew how honest they are and I figured that what is good for them is good for me."

Even the hostile government witnesses had to admit that the Socialist Workers Party members were always willing to help the unions. Stultz from Omaha was a hostile witness but, not being as shrewd as Bartlett, he admitted the truth. He testified that defendant Alfred Russell wrote letters for Local 554 in Omaha, that Russell helped negotiate with employers and that Russell and other members of the party edited a union paper to present the case of the workers to the public.

Party Members Help Workers

The workers in the union could not write and could not edit a paper because they did not have the benefits of a formal education. It is not their fault. It is the fault of a system that condemns youngsters to go to work at the age of 13 and 14; it is the fault of a system that prevents youngsters from attending high school and college. The employers had no difficulty in finding people who could write for them – they had money to hire such people – but the workers didn't have any money and so they had to depend upon members of the Socialist Workers Party, members who were willing to work for little or nothing in order to serve the interests of the workers. We admit that our members in helping workers always have in mind to convince the workers that the ideas of socialism are correct, but it is untrue that they go into the unions only with that purpose. They constantly have the welfare of the workers at heart.

Mr. Anderson naively asked the following question: "What business had the Socialist Workers Party to organize the Federal Workers Section? Should not the government be trusted with taking care of relief clients?" And by the government, I presume, Mr. Anderson means the people who have charge of WPA and the relief set-up. No, Mr. Anderson, it is obvious that the 2,000 members of the Federal Workers Section did not have sufficient confidence in the government officials. Out of these 2,000 members, there were probably no more than half a dozen or so members of the Socialist Workers Party. The fact that 2,000 men and women considered it necessary to become members of the Federal Workers Section proves conclusively that they thought the organization to be of great benefit to them. These men and women recognized that to protect their interests, it is necessary to organize and exert pressure upon government officials who otherwise would neglect their duties.

It has been the universal experience of all people that the government gives aid only to those people who are organized.

100

The farmers organize, and if they don't – they should. The same is true of the small business men. The workers organize and the unemployed have a right and a duty to organize.

The Defendants and Union Democracy

How did the members of our party who were in the leadership of Local 54 exercise control of the union? What is the policy of the Socialist Workers Party with reference to the method of controlling unions? You will find that policy explained in the **Declaration of Principles** and in the pamphlet on trade unionism written by Farrell Dobbs. Complete inner democracy in the trade unions is stressed both in the **Declaration** and in Dobbs' pamphlet.

Unfortunately there is very little democracy in the trade union movement. There is practically none where men like Tobin rule. But wherever the Socialist Workers Party members are elected to office, they see to it that the members of the union have full democratic rights.

We have a firm and undying conviction, ladies and gentlemen, that without the understanding cooperation of the masses of the people, there can be no progress; there can be no real progress if people do blindly what they are told to do, no matter how good the intentions of the leaders may be. There can be no real progress under the rule of dictators no matter how benevolent they may be. There can be progress only if the masses understand what they are doing, understand their rights and exercise those rights – only if the masses take control of their own fate and destiny – and this can be done only through education and the democratic process.

Some of you, when questioned by the Judge before being accepted as jurors, said that you had heard and read something about the Soviet Union and thought that it was a communistic or socialistic state. By this time I think you

101

understand that, as socialism is conceived by the defendants, its existence is impossible without freedom, without liberty, without democracy. There can be no socialism without freedom of the press, freedom of discussion, without the voluntary cooperation of the masses.

By the testimony of the government's witnesses it was shown that in Local 544, under the leadership of some of the defendants, there was complete democracy, complete honesty and the local was completely free of gangsterism and racketeerism except insofar as some of the government witnesses tried to get away with certain racketeering practices.

Oh yes, we were in favor of strikes. Mr. Anderson, in his opening statement, evidently with the intention of startling the jury, accused the defendants of never being satisfied, of constantly agitating for higher wages and more strikes, never wanting to arbitrate or to negotiate. But what has the evidence shown? The defendants, of course, have called strikes; but only after receiving authority from the members of the union, only after all attempts to negotiate with the employers had ended in failure. As far as Local 544 is concerned, the evidence shows that since 1936 there has not been a single major strike – the truck drivers were organized and the employers understood that they had to negotiate with Local 544.

Mr. Anderson also promised to show you that the defendants never believed in arbitration. But Mr. Dobbs, while he was on the witness stand, explained to you that while we prefer direct negotiations between unions and employers and while, as a general rule, we do not think arbitration is the best method of settling disputes, still we accept arbitration under certain circumstances. There is no question of principle involved.

When Mr. Dobbs said that he does not believe that there are impartial arbitrators, he explained that in a society divided into classes the fundamental issues dividing those classes cannot be arbitrated. There is no possibility of finding an impartial arbitrator on these fundamental issues. But that does not mean that we would exclude arbitration under all circumstances. The fact is that both in Local 541 and in the 11-state Over-the-Road Area Committee, when Mr. Farrell Dobbs was secretary, there were many cases of arbitration.

The evidence proves conclusively that the defendants practiced real trade union democracy to such an extent that the vast majority of the truck drivers followed the defendants and would now prefer them if they had a chance to indicate their preference by a democratic election.

Listing the Government Witnesses

In contrast to the trade union policy of the defendants, I shall now show you what was the trade union policy of the government witnesses. As indicated before, this case is nothing but a struggle between two factions in the union with the government siding with the faction consisting largely of the witnesses against the defendants. I will read you the names of the chief government witnesses and on the basis of their own testimony I think you must agree with me that they constitute the opposition to the leadership of the defendants in Local 544:

- James Bartlett – now organizer for 544-AFL.
- Eugene Williams – now organizer for 544-AFL.
- George O'Brien – now organizer for 544-AFL.
- Roy Wieneke – now organizer for 544-AFL.
- Tom McCue – now organizer for 544-AFL.
- Edward Blixt – now organizer for 544-AFL.
- Sidney Brennan – now Secretary-Treasurer of 544-AFL.

Those are the main witnesses. Then we come to witnesses of secondary rank: What is their relationship to the power that controls 544-AFL? They are:

103

- Walter K. Stultz – he and his wife are receiving pay from the Tobin Receiver of 554 in Omaha.
- Helen Hanifan – bookkeeper in 544-AFL.
- Harriet Karlen – stenographer of 544-AFL.

The following witnesses testified that they were formerly on the Tobin Receiver's payroll:

- Glen Smith – formerly organizer for the Receiver of 544-AFL, member of a squad. What kind of a squad, I think the jury understands. He was the man who beat up Jake Cooper and was proud of it. He did not deny there were 12 others with him at that time.
- Henry Harris – bodyguard for Bartlett.
- Jack Novack – member of what he claims to be a negotiating squad. That was the boy who obviously would be unable to negotiate anything with anybody.

The following government witnesses are the members of the Committee of 99, organized on behalf of Tobin to oppose the leadership of the defendants in 544:

- Karl Bath
- Robert Bove

Mr. Schweinhaut (Prosecutor): Bove was not a member of the Committee of 99.

Mr. Meyer (Defense Counsel): Look on page 1182 of the record, Mr. Schweinhaut.

Mr. Schweinhaut: I stand corrected.

Mr. Goldman: I continue the list:

- Elmer Buckingham
- E.G. Holstein
- John Majersky
- Joe Williams

104

All one has to do to become convinced that this trial is nothing but a continuation of the factional struggle in 544, is to read the names of the witnesses.

James Bartlett, Chief Witness

We must proceed now to analyze the testimony of some of the witnesses for the prosecution but I shall confine myself primarily, ladies and gentlemen, to only one witness. I confine myself largely to the witness who, in the words of Mr. Anderson, "continuously rose in stature during the trial until he reached way beyond the limit of the ceiling." Maybe I didn't understand Mr. Anderson correctly. Maybe he was only sarcastic.

There obviously are times in a man's life when he changes his opinions on important questions. I would be the last man in the world to attack anyone who, after spending a certain number of years in the socialist movement, finally reaches the conclusion that the movement is based on a wrong philosophy.

If James Bartlett were that type of man, I would, of course, regret his leaving the movement. But I would not attack him. If he were that type of man, he would never testify against us. He could not possibly be an honest man and testify as he did.

From his testimony Bartlett can be designated as a careerist – a man only interested in carving out a career for himself. He goes from one party to another, always with the idea in the back of his mind of assuring for himself a comfortable living.

Why does he claim he left the Socialist Workers Party? Because he found out that we were advocating force and violence. On the face of it, that is unbelievable.

Bartlett is a smart man – he is not an intelligent man –

but he is a smart fellow, there is no question about it. Under certain circumstances he would make a good business agent – better perhaps than most business agents. He can read. He testified that he wrote articles for the **Daily Worker**. He admitted that he read the **Communist Manifesto** before he joined the Communist Party. He admitted that he read **State and Revolution** by Lenin before he joined the Communist Party. When I asked him whether he knew that these two books advocated an armed overthrow of the government, he answered in the affirmative; that is, he knew that before he joined the Communist Party. He also admitted that he read a great deal of literature after he joined the Communist Party. He said he joined the Communist Party in 1932 and left it in the middle of 1933; and during this year and a half he read the literature of the party, he made speeches and wrote articles for the **Daily Worker**.

And then he states that he left the Communist Party because he found out that it advocated the violent overthrow of the government. So, after reading the **Communist Manifesto** and **State and Revolution**, the two documents which, in his opinion, advocated the violent overthrow of the government, it took him another year and a half to find out that the Communist Party advocated that doctrine!

Then in 1936 he comes to Mr. Vincent Dunne, and according to Bartlett's testimony, Mr. Dunne asks him to join the Socialist Workers Party. At that point I very quietly asked him: "Did Mr. Dunne tell you or give you to understand that the Trotskyists claimed to be the real Marxists as against the Stalinists?" Bartlett's answer was yes. Consider Mr. Bartlett's testimony! He says he left the Communist Party because he found out that it advocated the violent overthrow of the government. He comes to our party and knows, before joining our party, that we claim to be the real Marxists and he also testified that he read books by Marx and Lenin which, in his opinion, advocated the overthrow of the government by force

106

and violence. It must follow, then, from Bartlett's testimony that he should have known before he joined our party that we also advocated the violent overthrow of the government. But according to his testimony, it took him three years to find that out. He found that out early in 1940 when he left our party. He joined our party in 1936 or 1937; so it took Mr. Bartlett all these years to find that out.

Now, ladies and gentlemen, the dumb government witnesses who followed Bartlett – Novack, Harris and others whose names I don't remember – testified that at every party meeting they attended there was a discussion in which the violent overthrow of the government was advocated. Violet Williams testified that she attended many meetings, heard many lectures, did not remember the subject of the lectures or the contents of the lectures, but she remembered in general that we advocated the violent overthrow of the government. So we have people like Novack and Harris and Violet Williams – not very smart – and they find out that we advocate the violent overthrow of the government after attending two or three meetings.

Bartlett – the smart fellow who read the **Communist Manifesto** and **State and Revolution** before he joined the Communist Party in 1932, who, while in the Communist Party read all of the Communist Party literature and spoke for that party and wrote in the **Daily Worker,** who read many pamphlets while he was in our party – took three years before he found out that we advocate the violent overthrow of the government.

Mr. Anderson, for you to stand up now and say that you believe every word that Bartlett testified to would convict you of something more than sarcasm.

Let us go on. When, on cross-examination, I introduced certain statements made by Mr. Bartlett, I think that Mr. Schweinhaut and Mr. Anderson were overjoyed. It seemed that I had made a terrible blunder. I introduced the statement that

Bartlett made when he joined the Socialist Workers Party; also the statement that he made when he campaigned in his own union against an opposition; and also the letter that he had written to the **Star-Journal**. The gentlemen of the prosecution did not catch the significance of those statements that I introduced. I did not care what Bartlett said about himself in those statements. But what I was interested in was one assertion that he *didn't* make in any of these statements.

Bartlett claims, ladies and gentlemen, that he left the Communist Party because it advocated force and violence. Now, wouldn't it be natural to expect that if that were the truth, he would say so in the statement giving the reasons why he left the Communist Party? The only reason that he mentions now for his leaving the Communist Party, he never mentioned in the statement in which he explained why he left the Communist Party. Is there any sense in that?

When Bartlett issued the statement against some of our members who were running in opposition to him in the warehouse union elections, he had already left the Socialist Workers Party. And according to his testimony here he left the party because he found out that it advocated force and violence. Where, in the statement he wrote in 1940, is there any assertion of that kind? It isn't in that statement!

In the early part of this year Bartlett wrote a letter to the **Star-Journal**, a letter that I introduced in evidence. In it he claims that he left the Communist Party in the summer of 1934. But on the witness stand he testified that he left in 1933. It is obvious that he was lying on the witness stand, lying because he wanted to justify his further statement that during the 1934 strike he told Dunne he was out of the Communist Party. A liar, no matter how clever or how intelligent, finds it impossible to remember all the lies that he utters.

Why did he not, in the letter that he wrote to the **Star-Journal**, give as his reason for leaving the Socialist Workers

Party that it advocated the violent overthrow of the government? There is not a single mention of that. He never mentioned his alleged real reason for leaving the party in any of the statements that he made before this trial. In the parade of perjury represented by the government witnesses, Bartlett "rose to the ceiling" and way above it.

Mr. Anderson did not know that yesterday or the day before yesterday he, himself, convicted Bartlett of perjury. I shall show you how. Mr. Anderson was examining Mr. Dobbs. He had in his hand either the **ABC of Marxism** or **What Is Trotskyism** and he gleefully asked Mr. Dobbs: "Well, this was written in 1941, wasn't it?" Mr. Dobbs answered: "That is right."

When did Bartlett last visit the party headquarters? I asked him: "Was it March, was it February, was it April?" And finally he said that "It could not have been later than April 1940."

Then I had to maneuver carefully – because Bartlett is a smart fellow – to get him to admit that he bought **What Is Trotskyism** and the **ABC of Marxism** in the party headquarters. He stated definitely that he bought them in the headquarters.

Now, ladies and gentlemen, if the last time that Bartlett was at the headquarters was in April 1940 and if the pamphlets – as is proved by their internal context – were written after Trotsky's death, were published in February or March 1941, how could Bartlett get those two books in the headquarters? Try to solve that riddle, Mr. Anderson.

Is there any question but that Bartlett is a perjurer? Would any witness for the defense guilty of such perjury be permitted to be free at the present time? There would be an indictment out against him, but Bartlett is a government witness and the government wants to prove its case regardless of the evidence and Bartlett, the greatest perjurer and the greatest liar that ever sat in the federal court, is permitted to go free.

Friday, November 28, 1941
Afternoon Session

Perjury of Government Witnesses

The Court: You may proceed.

Mr. Goldman: Ladies and gentlemen, by this time you know enough about our theory to understand that it is difficult for me to speak with bitterness against any individual. By and large we hold that social conditions are responsible for the character of an individual and it is almost impossible for me as a Marxist to be bitter towards a government witness regardless of the depths of perjury which he reaches. That does not, of course, prevent me from pointing out the false testimony which the government witnesses gave.

Most of the important government witnesses – whose names I enumerated and who are directly or indirectly connected with the Tobin administration of Local 544-AFL – are helpless people who were motivated by a desire to get jobs in the local and they could do so only if the defendants were pushed out of their positions.

Those of the government witnesses who were former members of our party could testify to nothing about our program, with the exception, of course, that they testified that we advocated the armed overthrow of the government. I mentioned before that these people never remembered the subject or contents of a single pamphlet or party discussion, but always remembered that the defendants advocated the violent overthrow of the government. Mr. Eugene Williams, for instance, on direct examination remembered that Farrell Dobbs spoke at the first meeting he attended and naturally he also remembered that Farrell Dobbs advocated the armed overthrow of the government. On cross-examination he forgot that it was Farrell Dobbs and said that it was Felix Morrow, but still he remembered that, no matter who it was, the speaker advocated the armed overthrow of the government. And that's all he remembered.

Another significant point. A great many of the witnesses claimed that Vincent Ray Dunne who, as the outstanding leader of Local 544-CIO, is more or less of a chief devil in this picture, discussed with them the question of what our party wanted to do after the passing of the Selective Service Act. They testified that they had conversations with Dunne about this matter long after they were out of the party, even after they had fought in the union against our party members.

It looked peculiar, did it not, that Dunne who, you will all agree, is a highly intelligent person, should talk to people who were no longer members of the party and who were enemies of the party, about such delicate questions as inciting insurrection in the army. I think the jury must have seen the absurdity of that testimony.

Another piece of testimony that shows how much perjury the government witnesses really committed was their story that the executive board of the union paid Emil Hansen's weekly salary at the time he was acting as a guard for Leon Trotsky. This evidence, of course, could not possibly help the jury arrive at a decision as to whether or not the Socialist Workers Party conspired to overthrow the government by force and violence, but I presume the prosecution used it for some effect on the jury. But somebody had forgotten to coach Miss Hanifan, the bookkeeper of Local 544-AFL, and when I asked her: "Did you issue checks for Mr. Hansen when he was in Mexico?" she answered, "No." This admission came from a government witness and now I suppose the government will be forced to contend that Mr. Hansen was paid out of the cash box.

In and by itself a minor point like this is not worth much but when you take all the little and big falsehoods testified to by the government witnesses, you have before you a case based on witnesses whose testimony indicated one thing, and one thing only – they were not afraid of a possible prosecution for perjury.

Yesterday I argued that even if you considered the witnesses for the government as absolutely honest, you should disregard their testimony concerning statements allegedly made by the defendants two or three years ago because you have far more reliable, documentary evidence on which to base your decision. But you are not confronted with honest witnesses. On the contrary, you are confronted by witnesses who are now officially connected with Local 544-AFL – some of them paid organizers, most of them having taken the positions of the men who are now in the prisoners' dock – who were opposed to and fought the leadership of the defendants in 544 and whose testimony is shot through with falsehoods and perjury. There is nothing else for you to do but to give no credence whatever to this testimony.

Mr. Anderson made much of the fact that most of the testimony of these witnesses stood uncontradicted and undenied. This is a common trick used by lawyers. If a witness for one side makes 500 statements and the witness for the other side denies only 450 of them, then the other 50 undenied, prove the case. Suppose I had put all the defendants on the stand and all the defendants had denied all the statements which the government witnesses claimed they had made; wherein would that be of any help to you?

In this case, ladies and gentlemen, we are confronted with this situation: Either our program and our documents advocate the armed overthrow of the government by force and violence, in which case we are guilty; or else they do not advocate such a doctrine, in which case we are not guilty. The individual oral statements alleged to have been made by

113

defendants a year or two or three years ago should play no role. I do not try cases simply by denying statements attributed to defendants. I prefer to get to the very heart of the issue.

The charge in this case is conspiracy to overthrow the government by force and violence. Was there or was there not such a conspiracy? The government has introduced more than 150 exhibits consisting of articles, pamphlets and official declarations. Let the jurors determine their decision by those and not by isolated statements alleged to have been uttered by some of the defendants two or three years ago.

Real Motives of Witnesses

The government witnesses organized a Committee of 99 to fight socialism in Local 544. That is what they claim. Someone once said: "Patriotism is the last refuge of a scoundrel" and if ever this phrase applied, it applies to the government witnesses. These perjurers wrapped themselves in the American flag, not because they cared a tinker's damn about patriotism, but because in this way they think they can succeed in gaining a victory over the defendants. Their real motive was not to fight socialism but to get a few more dollars and get positions to which they could not be elected.

With great difficulty I succeeded in presenting the true motives of the government witnesses. It was the situation in the Minneapolis Brewery that gave the jury a clue as to their real motives. I do not intend to examine the evidence on that point in detail. You remember what the situation was there, the struggle between the executive board of the local composed largely of the defendants on the one hand, and government witnesses Holstein, Eugene Williams, Al Williams and Buckingham, on the other hand. You realized from the testimony of the government witnesses themselves that these people were participating in a racket. The government witness, Blixt, who worked in the market, was in a similar racket. When I asked

114

him whether, contrary to the orders of the executive board, he stopped farmers' trucks from coming into the market, he tried to excuse himself by saying that he stopped only the "wildcat" operators.

It was a great racket for these witnesses until the executive board of Local 544 stepped in and compelled them to give up this racket of charging small distributors, who wanted a load from the Minneapolis Brewery, a minimum of four hours' pay regardless of the time that it actually took to load the truck – whether it was 15 minutes or 20 minutes. You noticed that it was after the executive board compelled these witnesses to give up the racket that the Committee of 99 was organized to oppose the leadership of the union.

And this Committee of 99 could not convince the membership of 544, so the Committee invited the FBI to participate in its meetings. The FBI, in fact, became part of the Committee of 99. This testimony comes from the government's own witness and is uncontradicted.

Do not misunderstand me, ladies and gentlemen. I do not claim that the Committee of 99 was powerful enough to initiate and set into motion this prosecution – not Bartlett, not Tommy Williams, not these witnesses, oh no, men higher up, men who appointed a Receiver to take the defendants out of their jobs – these are the people who had the power to initiate and set into motion

Mr. Schweinhaut: That is absolutely not true, if your Honor please.

The Court: I don't think that is appropriate argument, Mr. Goldman; I don't think it is appropriate argument in the face of the state of this record, and I don't think you should pursue it.

Mr. Goldman: The Committee of 99 could not convince the members of Local 544 through argument. Is that in

115

the record? Witness after witness testified that they had a chance to run opposition candidates. That is in the record. Members of the Committee of 99 testified here one after another to this effect.

The Defendants Built the Union

"Under whose leadership was Local 544 organized?" I asked some of the government witnesses. They had to admit that the union was built by the Dunnes, Dobbs, Carl Skoglund, Harry DeBoer and everyone else who is a defendant and connected with Local 544. From a membership of 200, the defendants raised the local to 6,000. Do you think any of the government witnesses was capable of creating this powerful union that exerted tremendous influence throughout the northwest area? Who built the Over-the-Road Committee? Farrell Dobbs. And these government witnesses, members of the Committee of 99, some of them unfortunate half-wits, are now in the offices that the defendants had prior to Tobin's appointment of the Receiver.

"Were you elected to office?" I asked Sidney Brennan, who testified that he is now Secretary-Treasurer of 544-AFL. "No," he answered.

"Who appointed you?" "Neal," was the answer.

"You mean the Receiver for Tobin?" "Yes," was the answer.

Some of the government witnesses were at one time members of the Socialist Workers Party. What made these people join the party?

In commenting on the testimony of defendants Rainbolt and Orgon, Mr. Anderson said that had these defendants testified that they joined the party in order to get jobs, then he would have more consideration for them. Mr. Anderson doesn't see the significance of his remarks. He seems to think that the government witnesses who testified that they joined the party to get jobs have thereby cleansed themselves of any possible sin they committed by joining the party, while Mr. Rainbolt and Mr. Orgon are still criminals. The conclusion is: If people join the party because of idealistic reasons, because they are convinced that the party represents a cause worth fighting and dying for, then they belong in jail; but if they join the party in order to get a job, they should be released.

The defendants Rainbolt and Orgon did not know all the principles of the party when they joined. They joined because they knew the Dunnes; they knew Farrell Dobbs and Carl Skoglund and knew how honest these men were. Had there been, by the way, the slightest question of the honesty of the defendants in the leadership of 544, it would have surely been brought out in the evidence. No one dares impute any dishonest motives to any of the defendants.

Mr. Schweinhaut: Now, just a moment. I wish your Honor would instruct the jury that we could not have proved in evidence here that these men were dishonest except by criminal records, if any.

The Court: That is true. The jury will so heed that statement. Until a man proves his own character in evidence, it can't be impeached or criticized by the government.

Mr. Goldman: It is in evidence that the union executive board did not permit racketeering. It is in evidence that all these government witnesses who testified that they joined the party in order to get jobs in the union, didn't get jobs; that all the government witnesses who testified that they joined the party to hold their jobs, didn't hold their jobs. The government witnesses finally succeeded in getting jobs in the union, only when the defendants, who built the union by their blood and their sacrifices in the course of many strike struggles, were pushed out and are now threatened with deprivation of their

117

liberties. Take the testimony of all the members of the Committee of 99 and everything that I say will be borne out.

The government witnesses told the truth when they testified that they joined the Socialist Workers Party in order to get jobs. They probably thought that the Socialist Workers Party was like the Republican or Democratic Parties. They saw the defendants in charge of a union and they thought they could get jobs by joining the party of which the defendants were members. Quickly, however, they were disillusioned. They didn't get any jobs because men like the defendants don't put people into jobs in a union unless these people are capable.

Real Motives of Prosecution

The Committee of 99 covered up its real motives in the fight against the leadership of 544 by claiming to fight socialism. The prosecution likewise conceals its real motives.

Since January 1938 when the party was organized, we have been issuing a weekly paper, a monthly magazine and many pamphlets. I am sure that the all-powerful Federal Bureau of Investigation must have been aware of these facts known to many thousands of people. It was not, however, until July 15, 1941 that the Federal Government indicted the conspirators.

On June 9, 1941 the members of 544 decided to disaffiliate from the AFL and join the CIO. A little over a month after that, the indictment in this case was voted. The nearness of the two dates is a mere coincidence, the government claims, but it is certainly a very peculiar coincidence.

And why, pray, was the prosecution started in Minneapolis? The party headquarters is in New York. But the indictment was voted in Minneapolis and the government brought four of us from New York in order to cover up its real motives.

Was this case started in Minneapolis because a union defense guard was organized in Minneapolis? The fact is that in New York the party organized a workers' defense guard which actually fought with the fascists and Bundists on the streets. The conclusion is inevitable: the indictment was brought in Minneapolis where the activities of the leadership of Local 544 incurred the enmity of powerful persons with influence in Washington, especially the enmity of one person whose name I am not permitted to mention.

Grace Carlson was a candidate for senator in the fall of 1940. She spoke on the same platform with candidates from other parties. She spoke over the radio. Everyone heard her and not a single complaint was registered. Could it be presumed that the FBI and the whole government were asleep? No, that is not the explanation. The indictment came after the decision of Local 544 to secede from the AFL Teamsters International.

Mr. Schweinhaut: Are you willing to have me tell you why it was brought up, Mr. Goldman? [1]

Mr. Goldman: Sure, try to explain it. You cannot convince reasonable people, who know that for three and a half years the party carried on its activities openly and with its headquarters in New York, that there is any other explanation for bringing the prosecution in Minneapolis and at this time, except as a result of the fight in Local 544.

How the Courts Function

One piece of evidence I must mention because it was introduced by the government only for the purpose of prejudicing the jury. It was my article on the federal courts. Perhaps the government will contend that because I do not think the courts have as their purpose the protection of working-class interests, I am therefore to be considered as one who would want to overthrow the government by force and violence.

119

I said in that article that under the present system the courts could not possibly give as fair a trial to a poor man as to a wealthy man. I didn't blame the situation on the individual judge; I placed the blame upon the system. A judge may be as fair as any human being can possibly be and yet when he fines a wealthy man $200 and a poor man $200, there can in reality be no equality between the two fines. It is not a question of the intention of a judge but of the operation of a system. I think that in the article introduced in evidence I gave an example of a case where certain oil companies indicted under the Anti-Trust Laws were fined $5,000 and certain workers participating in a strike fined $500. It was not difficult for an oil company to pay $5,000 but imagine how difficult it was for a worker to raise $500. The injustice lies in the social system which the courts mirror.

We proclaim that men are born equal but can it be said that the child born in a wealthy family, with all advantages assured him, is equal to the child born in poverty, deprived of the possibility of getting proper food and a decent education?

The Rank-and-File Defendants

I do not intend to consider in detail the evidence against the individual defendants. You already know that I have not conducted the case on the basis that some defendants may be more guilty than others. Still, as a lawyer not only for myself but for all the defendants, I wish to point out that the evidence against some of the defendants could not possibly justify a verdict of guilty, even if you should consider that the party is guilty of conspiring to overthrow or to advocate the overthrow of the government by force and violence. The government is obligated to prove, beyond a reasonable doubt, that each one of the defendants not only joined the so-called conspiracy but knew the nature and object of the conspiracy. As far as I am concerned, as far as Jim Cannon and Farrell Dobbs and others who rightly can be considered leaders of the party are concerned, we stand on the proposition that there could not possibly have been any conspiracy to overthrow the government by force and violence or to advocate the overthrow of the government by force and violence. We stand on the proposition that our program, if rightly interpreted and correctly construed, does not and cannot mean that we are guilty of this kind of a conspiracy.

But who knows? Perhaps all that I say about our program will not avail us and I must therefore try to save from the clutches of the government those people who cannot be considered leaders of the party, who joined, not because they read the literature of our party, but because from bitter experience they learned the truth of our fundamental principles, namely that in this world there is a class that produces the wealth of society and a class that gets all the benefit of that wealth. These members are not acquainted with all the theories of Marx but they are, as we call them, class-conscious. The government has not proved, beyond a reasonable doubt, that every defendant knew and understood the nature of our program or the nature of the so-called conspiracy.

The fact that the government witnesses testified about certain defendants – that they said this or that about armed revolution – does not prove that those defendants knew the program. You must consider all the evidence from this angle: Did the government prove, beyond a reasonable doubt, that the defendants were members of the conspiracy and knew the object and nature of the conspiracy?

The second count in the indictment is based on a statute which was passed June 28, 1940. Did the government succeed in proving that all of the defendants were members of the conspiracy subsequent to that date?

This, of course, is a minor matter, but after all, if you believe the preposterous contention of the government that we advocated the overthrow of the government by force and violence, then you must make the government prove, beyond a reasonable doubt, that all the defendants were members of the party subsequent to June 28, 1940. And the government must also prove that all the defendants had knowledge of the nature and object of the conspiracy. The government undoubtedly proved that the leaders knew what the party stood for, but in a legal sense they did not prove that all the defendants knew and understood the principles of the party.

Government Denies Rights to SWP Members

If you accept the theory of the government with reference to the activities of the defendants, then you have this peculiar situation, that a person who becomes a member of the Socialist Workers Party has no right to do anything at all which every other citizen has a right to do.

A person living in the United States has a right to join a union and to participate in the activities of the union. A member of the Socialist Workers Party cannot join a union and participate in its activities because if he does, it will be used against him as evidence that he was a member of a conspiracy to overthrow the government.

Other people have a right to oppose the country's entry into the war now raging in Europe, but if a member of the Socialist Workers Party opposes the war, he is immediately subject to the charge of conspiring to overthrow the government by force and violence.

The government has introduced evidence covering a great many activities of the defendants. What follows from this? A member of the Socialist Workers Party cannot be active in a trade union; he cannot oppose the war; he cannot propose the creation of a workers' defense guard to defend unions against fascist bands; he cannot possibly go hunting because he would have to purchase a rifle and that would be evidence of conspiracy.

Reporters, journalists, politicians, authors could go to Mexico for the purpose of seeing Trotsky, but not a member of the Socialist Workers Party because his visit to Trotsky would be introduced into evidence against him.

A member of the Socialist Workers Party cannot advise people to read Marx or Engels or Lenin. Professors at the universities can do so but not members of the Socialist Workers Party. A member of the Socialist Workers Party cannot go to a New Year's affair, organized by the Socialist Workers Party. Everyone else can attend such affairs but not members of the Socialist Workers Party, for that constitutes evidence against members.

A member of the Socialist Workers Party went to Mexico and attended a bull fight, and it is introduced here as evidence against him. Perhaps because he may have learned the art of handling a sword and that would be evidence of a conspiracy to overthrow the government by force and violence.

A member of the Socialist Workers Party has therefore only one right and that is to sit in jail and I presume even in jail he could be charged with a conspiracy to destroy the jail and the government. When Mr. Anderson, in his argument, made a statement that the Socialist Workers Party could do nothing that is right, he practically said what I am contending at present: that a member of our party has no rights except to be in jail.

Concrete Proof of Our Prediction

I must for a moment, ladies and gentlemen, go back to the question of whether we advocate the violent overthrow of the government, or simply predict that the social revolution will be accompanied by violence exercised by the minority. I want to give you an example taken from the evidence, proving that our prediction will undoubtedly be fulfilled and also proving that they who want to put us in jail because of our ideas are the very ones who use violence.

You heard Sidney Brennan testify that he is Secretary-Treasurer of Local 544. He admitted that he was not elected to that office, that he was appointed by Neal, Tobin's Receiver. He admitted that the defendants were elected to office in Local 544 in the elections of January of this year. There was a fair election, a secret ballot and no one contested that election.

Who, ladies and gentlemen, practiced democracy in 544? Who used the ballot in order to get power in 544? The defendants.

Who are now in office in 544, ladies and gentlemen? The defendants who were elected? No, Sid Brennan, Bartlett and the other witnesses who could never get elected to office but who were appointed by Tobin's Receiver.

Who practiced violence, ladies and gentlemen? Tobin's goon squads. Who took defendants Roy Orgon and Jake Cooper off their jobs and beat up Jake Cooper? The minority who couldn't and didn't get elected to office in 544 organized their forces and exercised violence against the defendants who were elected to office and against the rank and file who elected the defendants to office.

And we make the same prediction with reference to the change of the social order. The defendants will get a majority to accept their ideas and the minority, determined to retain their power and their privileges, will be the ones to use violence.

In the case of Local 544 there was no possibility of answering violence with violence. Against the state government, against the federal government, against the goon squads, the defendants were helpless. We had to submit, but if there is anything that proves our contention that violence will come from a minority, it is this very example of what occurred in Local 544.

Why didn't the government give the truck drivers of 514 a little democracy? Why didn't the government suppress the violence of the minority? Why didn't the government see to it that the truck drivers obtained the right of having the union of their choice? Hypocrisy and nothing else characterizes the case for the government! Frame-up and nothing else! The government is part of the Committee of 99 and belongs to the faction led by one whom I am not permitted to mention.

That, ladies and gentlemen, is the heart and the essence of this case.

The Court: I think, Mr. Goldman, that we will have a short recess.

(Afternoon Recess)

We Fight for a New World

Mr. Goldman: Ladies and gentlemen, you see before you defendants who are here in this courtroom because they are dissatisfied. Dissatisfied not with their personal fortunes, but with the social system, with the evils that exist under the present social order.

I presume that by and large the defendants could, if they wanted to, solve their own problems in a very satisfactory manner. And perhaps we ought to be in jail because, instead, we have spent our lives defending what we think to be ideas that can solve the problems of mankind. As for myself, who knows, maybe I could be a district attorney, perhaps even a judge. Perhaps Jim Cannon would be far better off personally if he thought and acted the way most people think and act. But all of us represent that type of person who does not think very much about his personal fortunes but thinks of mankind, of society in general.

The agony, the death of millions of human beings in senseless wars are not abstractions to us. We feel them keenly and we react to them and we try to create a world where destruction and war and poverty and disease will not be the lot of man.

We have studied and our studies have led us to certain conclusions and we have banded together to propagate those conclusions. We proclaim to the world that it is possible to build a new social order guaranteeing every human being a decent livelihood and a chance to develop his individuality, free from economic worries, free from the dangers of war. We say that we have reached an epoch where mankind must go forward to socialism or else back to barbarism.

With great effort and amidst tremendous suffering, man has traveled throughout the centuries in the direction of a better world. Men have laid down their lives by the millions so that future generations might cross over their bodies to achieve a world of greater freedom and more happiness. And throughout all history there have been men and women a little ahead of the procession telling the masses to proceed in a certain direction and to struggle for a larger share of the things that they create. And these men who have led the procession have had to pay for it – the prophets, Christ, Marx, Lenin, Trotsky – these are the men who fought for a new world and against them have always been arrayed the powers that be, the priests and Pharisees.

When Pilate said, "I found no fault in this man," the priests became more furious and said, "He stirreth up the people throughout all Judea."

"He stirreth up the people" – almost the exact words that Mr. Anderson used against us when he said we stir up the people. And we cannot deny that we tried to stir up the people.

We try to bring them a message of hope that a new world is possible and can easily be created if only they take their fight into their own hands, a new world where war and destruction will be unknown. But as I have indicated to you, all our stirrings, all our messages, will be in vain unless we are correct in our general analysis, unless we are correct in our theory that the social system has reached a point of decline where no road other than the road to socialism will lead mankind into a peaceful world. All our pamphlets, all our papers, all our speeches will be for naught unless we are correct in our fundamental theory, and if we are correct in our fundamental theory, all the efforts of the prosecution to silence our voice will not avail.

The prosecutors, and those that give them orders, do not understand that to thwart our agitation it is only necessary for them to solve the problems of mankind. Do they think that by silencing the voices of a few agitators they can satisfy the people who will suffer the agonies of war and of the hunger that will come with economic dislocation after the war?

Mr. Anderson, in his opening speech, referred to the attempts of the defendants to destroy organized society. Imagine calling a society "organized" that permits millions of human beings to be slaughtered, that permits poverty in the midst of plenty, that permits the spiritual and physical violence that exists throughout the universe! Chaos and destruction and death are not characteristics of an "organized" society.

The strength of our ideas lies in the very fact that we are living in a thoroughly unorganized society. The strength of our ideas lies in the fact that our general predictions, based upon the laws operating in society, must inevitably come true. At the beginning of the First World War we said that it would not solve any of the problems confronting the peoples. Who can deny that we were right? And now we say to the people of this country, "This war which your leaders claim is a war for democracy against fascism will not solve any of your problems because if the capitalist system is permitted to endure, the inevitable result will be fascism and more wars."

We base our activities upon a theory that has withstood the test of time and events. In the midst of a catastrophic war that will necessarily envelop the whole world, in the midst of the roar of cannons and the shrieking of shells, amidst the sobs and the wailing of mothers, amidst tears and blood, we still have hopes that the people will come to accept the ideas of socialism. The darkness that surrounds us can be dissipated only by the sun of socialism.

What Your Verdict Will Mean

No matter what your verdict is, it will be a historic one. Should it be guilty, then it will be an aid to reaction. It will, to that extent, aid the powers that are interested in preventing a change in the social order. It will not bring to a stop the struggle that is going on in society because, as I have indicated to you many times before, that struggle is a result of social conditions and not of our agitation.

A verdict of not guilty will mean that to that extent you are unwilling to lend your aid to the forces of reaction, that you are determined to live up to the Bill of Rights guaranteeing every minority in this country the right to free speech and free press.

We do not ask you to agree with our ideas. We have not asked you to do so once throughout this trial. We ask you only to understand these ideas and therefore to understand that we are not guilty of the charges leveled against us by the government. By a verdict of not guilty you will not only guard the constitutional rights of all minorities but you will help transform this chaotic world in a peaceful way.

The more democracy we have, the greater the chances

are for a peaceful transformation. Do away with democracy, and violence will surely accompany the social revolution. What more can I ask of you than by your verdict to guard the Bill of Rights and thus help prevent the plague which is threatening to destroy civilization, the plague of fascism.

Permit me to say once more and in conclusion: Our ideas, a product of existing conditions, are indestructible. They will ultimately conquer the minds and the hearts of the masses who will struggle for their realization because there is no road to peace and plenty other than the road of socialism.

Note

1. Assistant Attorney-General Schweinhaut, who followed Goldman in the final argument, never tried to explain it.